KT-431-818

# HOW TO RAISE AN OX

# HOW TO RAISE AN OX

## ZEN PRACTICE AS TAUGHT
## IN ZEN MASTER DOGEN'S SHOBOGENZO
### INCLUDING TEN NEWLY TRANSLATED ESSAYS

by

# FRANCIS DOJUN COOK

## FOREWORD BY TAIZAN MAEZUMI ROSHI

CENTER PUBLICATIONS, LOS ANGELES CALIF.

OTHER TITLES AVAILABLE FROM CENTER PUBLICATIONS:

*Zen Writings Series*

*On Zen Practice: Foundations of Practice*
*On Zen Practice II: Body, Breath and Mind*
*To Forget the Self: An Illustrated Guide to Zen*
 *Meditation*
*The Hazy Moon of Enlightenment: On Zen Practice III*
*The Way of Everyday Life*
*Sayings and Doings of Pai-chang* (1979)

*HOW TO RAISE AN OX* IS PUBLISHED UNDER THE JOINT AUSPICES OF THE ZEN CENTER OF LOS ANGELES AND THE INSTITUTE FOR TRANSCULTURAL STUDIES. FOR FURTHER INFORMATION, CONTACT: CENTER PUBLICATIONS, 905 S. NORMANDIE AVENUE, LOS ANGELES, CALIFORNIA 90006 © 1978 BY ZEN CENTER OF LOS ANGELES, INC. PRINTED IN THE UNITED STATES OF AMERICA.

LIBRARY OF CONGRESS CATALOGING IN PUBLICATION DATA:

COOK, FRANCIS DŌJUN
 HOW TO RAISE AN OX

 BIBLIOGRAPHY, P. 90.
 1. DŌGEN, 1200–1253. SHŌBŌGENZŌ. 2. SŌTŌSHŪ—DOCTRINES.
I. DŌGEN, 1200–1253. SHŌBŌGENZŌ. SELECTIONS. ENGLISH. 1978
II. TITLE.
BQ9449-D654553325 294.3'4'4 78-12025
ISBN 0-916820-07-6

*This book is dedicated with deep respect and gratitude to*
*Daiun Sōgaku Harada Roshi, Hakuun Ryōko Yasutani Roshi,*
*and Baian Hakujun Kuroda Roshi, splendid exemplars of*
*the lineage of Zen Master Dōgen.*
*Thanks to their grandfatherly kindness and compassion,*
*we now all have a better chance to learn to raise an ox.*

# CONTENTS

The Zen master Yüan-chih (Ta-an) of Chang-ching Hall in Fu country once addressed the monks in the Dharma hall: "For thirty years I lived on Mt. Wei and during that time I ate the monastery's rice and gave it back in the latrine. I did not learn the Zen of Master Wei-shan. All I did was raise a water buffalo. When he wandered from the path into the grass, I pulled him back; when he ran amuck in someone's garden, I chastised him with a whip. Now he has been tame for some time. Unfortunately, he used to pay too much attention to what people said, but now, however, he has become a pure white domesticated bull. He is always right in front of me wherever I am, dazzling white all day long, and even if I try to drive him away, he will not go." We should pay careful attention to this story. The thirty years of arduous practice with the patriarch [Wei-shan] consisted of eating rice, and there was no other consideration. When you realize the meaning of the life of eating rice, you will also understand the deep meaning of raising the buffalo bull.

from *Shōbōgenzō Kajō*

# FOREWORD

It can be said that the writings of Dōgen Zenji are among the highest achievements not only of Japanese but even of world literature. The esteem in which his work is held stems at least in part from its multiple levels of purpose and meaning. When we appreciate his work as literature, it displays true poetic mastery, while many of his essays serve admirably as criticism. Viewed philosophically, it is a near-perfect expression of truth, while from a moral/ethical standpoint, the absolute goodness and righteousness of which the human race is capable are beautifully expressed. Perhaps most cogently, as a body of religious work we see in it that excellent state of well-accomplished enlightenment which far transcends the duality of good and evil which we normally discuss.

Dogen Zenji's expression is like an inexhaustible spring which gushes out of the ground naturally and without impediment. Indeed, so freely does his wisdom spring forth that readers often feel almost lost as they read, nearly drowning in that fountain's endless flow.

Amidst such richness and subtlety, the task of translation and interpretation might overwhelm most scholars, both Eastern and Western. The demands of Dogen Zenji's language and insight are indeed rigorous, and present formidable challenges to translator and interpreter alike.

It is most fortunate that Dr. Cook has done this work. Highly respected in academic and scholarly circles, he is presently serving as director of academic studies at the Institute for Transcultural Studies in Los Angeles, and has held faculty posts at Dartmouth College and the University of California at Riverside, where he is an associate professor in the Religious Studies program. His previous publications include *Hua Yen Buddhism: The Jewel Net of Indra* (1977, Pennsylvania State University Press); a translation of Fa-tsang's *A Brief Commentary On The Heart Sutra* (1978, publ. in *Buddhist Meditation In Theory And Practice*, University of Hawaii Press); and numerous articles in scholarly and learned journals. Dr. Cook is also an authority on Whiteheadian process philosophy.

As a translator, Dr. Cook's masterful command of the Japanese language was enriched by his experience as a Fulbright Fellow in 1966–68, while studying at Kyoto University. Beyond language skills, Dr. Cook has been devotedly practicing Zen meditation for ten years, which affords him an experiential base from which he can speak with considerable authority. Going beyond the mere intellectualizing and speculation which so sharply limit much contemporary Zen scholarship, his translations and interpretations can be solidly relied upon by the scholar and the practitioner alike.

He has chosen well from the ninety-five chapters of Dogen's masterwork, the *Shobogenzo*, to present some of the central aspects of practice as Dogen Zenji experienced and transmitted it.

I shall not attempt to add to what he has already expressed so well in the first half of this book. Rather, I should like to encourage the reader himself to personally experience, interpret, and evaluate what Dr. Cook says in this excellent translation and interpretation of Dogen Zenji's work. Having read about how to raise an ox, the next step, naturally, is to raise one.

Hakuyu Taizan Maezumi
Los Angeles
September, 1978

# PREFACE

My function in bringing these chapters of *Shōbōgenzō* to the attention of Western readers has been merely that of a kind of midwife. The splendor and beauty of the baby is not at all my doing but is the contribution of the mother. I offer this volume in the hope that it will be carefully read and studied and that my fellow Westerners will come to appreciate the magnificent work of Dōgen Zenji as I have. My primary objective is to help the reader to gain a better understanding of what it means to practice Zen, particularly in the Sōtō form established by Dōgen Zenji.

The study of the right kind of literature can contribute greatly to Zen practice. In the application of zazen to everyday life, which is one of the most important features of Zen training, everything one does comes to be zazen. This applies to reading and study too, if the literature is not trivial or distracting. In the world of Zen training, where there is neither good nor bad, reading and study are no better or worse than any other activity. Westerners, and particularly Americans, who have developed many wrong notions about Zen, need to relinquish the comfortable and self-serving idea that reading and study are bad for one's spiritual health. This notion is the result of a misunderstanding of the relationship between Zen and literary activity and has been aggravated by an intellectual carelessness on the part of many who develop an interest in Zen. Zen should not be used as an excuse for sloppiness or laziness, which are very un-Zen. We need to recall that the library was one of the buildings of Zen monastic compounds in Chinese Buddhism and that Dōgen Zenji included a library in his own monastery. He also wrote a list of monastic rules, called *shingi*, which prescribe in minute detail how one should comport oneself in the monastery, and many rules have to do with respect for books. The right literature—and *Shōbōgenzō* is included in this category—can do much to clarify what good practice is and is not, point out dangers in one's practice, and most of all, inspire one to practice diligently. Each of us needs this constant inspiration to practice in the very best way we can. The teacher does much to inspire us, but so do other people, reflection on impermanence, dissatisfaction with the quality of our life, and many other things. A work such as *Shōbōgenzō*, in its discussion of practice, in its examples of great Zen masters, and particularly in the example of Dōgen Zenji himself, offers us one of the very finest sources for this inspiration and encouragement. I do not see how anyone could read what Dōgen Zenji has to say about Zen practice and not have some of Dōgen Zenji's spirit rub off on him and be encouraged by it.

# ONE

## *Introduction*

The Zen of Dōgen is the Zen of practice. Whatever else
may be said about the ninety-five chapters of his *Shōbōgenzō*—and there is so much that can be said—it is clear that
the main theme that runs through these chapters is that of the
necessity for daily, serious, continuous practice of Zen at all ✓
times. It may seem redundant to speak of Zen in this way, but
in making the claim, something special is intended which
highlights Dōgen's understanding of what it means to "learn
the Way." To understand what it means to say that Dōgen's
Zen is the Zen of practice is to understand something of that
remarkable man's place in the development of Buddhism, as
well as something of the nature of Buddhism in general. It is
my earnest hope that these translations of the nine chapters
from *Shōbōgenzō* and of *Fukan zazengi* will help to clarify what
he stood for and what he had to say.

Western students of Buddhism these days are not quite so
prone to make the errors of interpretation that characterized

earlier generations, but there still remains a tendency to misunderstand certain aspects of Buddhism. For instance, it is generally said that the goal of Buddhism is enlightenment. In a sense, this is true, but it is misleading when it is claimed without qualification. It might be more accurate to say that in Mahayana Buddhism, enlightenment is the doorway through which one must necessarily pass in order to reach the true goal. Also, it is generally understood that enlightenment is a sudden, dramatic, self-transforming event which occurs only after a long preparatory period of moral self-cleansing and hard meditation, but this is not exactly the way it was understood by Dōgen and many of his Chinese predecessors. Also, along with this, it is assumed that this enlightenment is a one-time event, the prize which is finally claimed after much practice and which terminates that practice. If practice exists for the sake of enlightenment, why practice once the prize is won? But the Zen masters tell us repeatedly that there is nothing to attain. Furthermore, this "nothing" is attained many times in varying degrees of intensity and depth, as the biography of the Zen master Hakuin shows. Finally, there is a pervasive tendency to equate Buddhist enlightenment with Western varieties of mysticism, though a careful reading of *Shōbōgenzō* indicates that such a category may be inappropriate for the experience that is Dōgen's primary concern. With all due respect and, truly, much good will towards my Christian friends who wish to find close similarities between Dōgen Zenji and, say, Theresa of Avila in the spirit of ecumenical good will, I feel more and more that the differences are indeed great. Bodhidharma put his finger on it when he answered Emperor Wu's question about the holy meaning of Buddhism by saying, "Vast emptiness, and nothing holy about it."

When I characterize Dōgen's Zen as the Zen of practice, I am not suggesting that his form of Buddhism is the only one concerned with practice. All forms of Buddhism necessarily involve practice because Buddhism *is* mainly practice. It is a markedly experiential religion inasmuch as the true life in the Dharma involves a realization (i.e., a making real) of those doctrines taught by the historical Buddha, and this making real does not happen in the absence of constant effort, which is the daily, regular, conscious direction of the will to that realization. Without this effort, Buddhism would degenerate into mere philosophy, or into the routine, customary profession of faith, or into vague, warm feelings directed towards some remote, mysterious Other. Rinzai Zen is certainly a Buddhism of practice, and so are Shingon, Tendai, and Pure Land Buddhism. Anyone who has spent time in a meditation center in Burma or Thailand knows that Theravada Buddhism is also a Buddhism of practice, and a rather demanding one at that. To say that Dōgen's Zen is the Zen of practice does not at all mean that no other form of Buddhism is concerned with practice. Something else is intended. It is partially indicated by some traditional terms which have been used to point out the unique features of Dōgen's Zen.

*Honshō myōshū* means "wonderful practice based on intrinsic enlightenment." It is an important phrase because it embodies two ideas which are central to Dōgen's understanding of Buddhism. *Honshō* ("intrinsic enlightenment")refers to the idea that all living beings are Buddhas. It does not mean that beings possess a Buddha nature, or that beings are containers in which a seed form of Buddha can be found, as if there were two realities, beings and Buddha. It means that beings are Buddhas, but they are blind, stupid Buddhas who are ignorant of their true nature. Second, the whole phrase, *honshō myōshū*, points to the manner in which beings should proceed to make this hidden nature manifest and functional. It means that practice should not be undertaken in the mistaken notion that it has a purely instrumental value, as a means to a separate and presumably greater end. To believe that one does zazen now in order to acquire enlightenment later is to merely perpetuate and strengthen the very dualisms that lie at the root of the human problem. It tacitly assumes that there is a difference between beings and Buddha, means and ends, and now and then. Moreover, to use practice in such a way encourages the very greed and attachment human beings seek to escape, for the eager pursuit of self-spiritualization is in fact just one more attempt by beings to achieve self-gratification. Primarily, the belief that practice culminates in enlightenment is a denial of what was for Dōgen the basis for his own achievement—the conviction that all beings just as they are are Buddhas.

The second phrase is *shūshō ittō,* which means "the one-ness *(ittō)* of practice *(shū)* and enlightenment *(shō).*" *Shūshō ittō* also points the way to correct practice because it cautions us not to think of enlightenment as a future event which will result from present practice. Instead, we must proceed in the knowledge that we are already that which we hope to become, and that our practice is the external appearance of this inherent enlightenment. In actuality, it is not even we as sentient beings who engage in the practice, it is the Buddha we are who practices. Consequently, there is no sequence of before and after, ordinary beings now, Buddhas later. When we truly practice Zen, we are being Buddhas with no question of a later payoff for our investment in practice. Practice and enlightenment are the same; to practice is to be a Buddha.

When Dōgen Zenji returned to Japan after his trip to China, the first thing he wrote was *Fukan zazengi* ("General Recommendations for Doing Zazen"), and in it he said, "Do not sit [i.e., do zazen] in order to become a Buddha, because that has nothing to do with such things as sitting or lying down." This warns us not to think that Buddhahood results from practice. We recall the famous dialogue between Master Huai-jang and Ma-tsu, whom Huai-jang found doing zazen. When asked why he was doing it, Ma-tsu replied, "To become a Buddha." Thereupon, Huai-jang sat down and began to polish a piece of brick. "Why are you polishing that brick?" asked Ma-tsu. "I'm going to turn it into a mirror," was the master's answer. "But," said Ma-tsu, "no amount of polishing

4

will turn that brick into a mirror." "That is true," replied
Huai-jang, "and no amount of zazen will turn you into a
Buddha, either." This story is not meant to deny the necessity
of practice. Practice is essential, the heart of Buddhism and
the key to learning the Way, but it should not be a calculating,
scheming means to an end. True practice is the enlightened
activity of the Buddha we already are.

Dōgen's understanding of practice turns the older, traditional Buddhist sequence of morality, meditation, and enlightenment *(śīla, samādhi, prajñā)* upside down. In the
Buddhism prior to his time, it was taught that a proper observance of moral and ethical injunctions was the necessary,
preliminary basis for the central practice of meditation. The
rationale for this apparently is the obvious one, that a person
who is careless in his interpersonal relationships is just not
the kind of person who can meditate effectively. Thus, the
order of morality and meditation seems ultimately to have
had a practical basis. Then meditation led to insight and enlightenment. However, Dōgen places enlightenment first, as
the basis of both meditation and ethics, and these latter two
are then considered to be based on prior enlightenment, or,
better, they are manifestations of prior enlightenment.
Dōgen's views on the matter of ethics or morality led him to
the conclusion that a set of ethical precepts imposed from the
outside and obeyed as a set of actions that ought to be followed was unrealistic, even futile. Rather, he felt the only
real, practical observance of the precepts had to be an organic
unfolding of a mode of conduct which was itself an expression of an enlightened nature. In fact, Dōgen says that
ethics and meditation are the same thing. "When one does
zazen, what ethical precepts are not being observed?" he asks.
How this is so will become clearer as I say something more
specific about Dōgen's definition of zazen. Ethics and meditation are thus both "wonderful practice based on intrinsic enlightenment." It is wonderful because it is natural, innate
nature appearing in the world of events. It is, in fact, the life

of the Buddha. The historical Buddha was called *Tathāgata* ("he who comes from the ultimate nature") because as a realized Buddha he was simply the appearance in the conditioned world of this enlightened activity.

The idea that meditation, ethics, and enlightenment are all the same thing was not exactly Dōgen's innovation. The story about the brick polishing indicates that Dōgen's Chinese predecessors had already understood this relationship. It was apparently the outcome of the doctrine of "intrinsic enlightenment," which was emphasized in Chinese Buddhism and is in fact one of its most obvious characteristics. This doctrine of intrinsic enlightenment is, in Dōgen's teaching, raised up to the status of the central and crucial fact, and it explains his whole approach to training in the Dharma. For Dōgen, it is not even really correct to say that it is the ordinary human being who is performing the practice; it is the Buddha we already are who instigates the practice and maintains it. "No ordinary being ever became a Buddha," he says in *Yuibutsu yobutsu*, "only Buddhas become Buddhas."

The first clear statement of this insight occurs in the *Platform Sutra* of Hui-neng, the sixth patriarch of Chinese Zen. It is clear that there is continuity between Hui-neng's Zen and Dōgen's Zen. Hui-neng says,

> Good friends, my teaching of the Dharma takes meditation *(ting)* and wisdom *(hui)* as its basis. Never under any circumstances mistakenly say that meditation and wisdom are different; they are a unity, not two things. Meditation itself is the substance of wisdom; wisdom itself is the function of meditation. At the very moment when there is wisdom, then meditation exists in wisdom; at the very moment when there is meditation, then wisdom exists in meditation. Good friends, this means that medita-

tion and wisdom are alike. Students, be
careful not to say that meditation gives rise
to wisdom, or that wisdom gives rise to meditation, or that meditation and wisdom are
different from each other. To hold this view
implies that things have duality. . . .[1]

The point that Hui-neng wished to make here is that what
seem to be two things are in fact one and the same. For
Dōgen, too, they are identical, and so the duality of means
and ends is overcome and the way to correct practice is
shown. To sit upright with straight back, with mind and body
unified, empty and unattached to internal and external
events, this is itself Buddha wisdom, Buddha mind.

"Buddha-tathāgatas," says Dōgen, "all have a wonderful
means, which is unexcelled and free from human agency, for
transmitting the wondrous Dharma from one to another
without alteration and realizing supreme and complete
awakening. That it is only transmitted without deviation
from buddha to buddha is due to the *jijuyū* samādhi, which is
its touchstone."[2] *Jijuyū samādhi* is another important term. It
is synonymous with zazen, and to understand the meaning of
the term may help to make clear why Dōgen Zenji stresses
practice as he does. *Ji* means "self" or "oneself", and *ju* and *yū*
mean "receive" and "use", respectively. The samadhi called
*jijuyū*, therefore, is meditation which one enjoys and uses for
oneself. It is contrasted with *tajuyū samādhi*, which is samadhi
performed for someone else or some other purpose, such as
for other beings or in order to acquire Buddhahood. Rather
than do zazen for these reasons, one sits quietly, without
expectation, in jijuyu samadhi simply to enjoy the nature
which is inherently one's own. Here there is no question of
means and ends, but only enjoying our true nature. This
zazen practice is, according to Dōgen's *Fukan zazengi*, zazen
in which we "gauge our enlightenment to the fullest."

According to Dōgen, Śākyamuni himself first enjoyed

this samadhi while sitting under the bodhi tree for several days after his own realization. There was no question of using the samadhi for some ulterior purpose, because he had already obtained everything there was to obtain. Then why did he continue to sit in jijuyu samadhi? He was just enjoying his Buddahood. But eventually he rose and went on to teach his Dharma for the next forty-five years, for jijuyu samadhi is not completely separate from tajuyu samadhi, samadhi used for the benefit of others. Sentient beings are numberless, and the Buddhist, if he truly follows the Mahayana Way, must arouse the determination to do whatever is in his power to emancipate all these sentient beings by leading them to the other shore. Consequently, while jijuyu samadhi is simultaneously the tajuyu samadhi which is put to the service of the infinitely numerous other, the proper orientation in samadhi is at once a realistic acknowledgement of the source of this other-directed activity and a way to avoid a self-defeating tendency to think dualistically.

If one is in fact a Buddha right now, why practice at all? Isn't it enough that we are told by scripture and personal testimony that we are, always have been, and always will be Buddhas? This was the question which plagued the young Dōgen and eventually led him to China in search of the right answer. The answer itself is not really difficult to find but it is vitally important that it is thoroughly understood. We are Buddhas, but for most, this is not real knowledge. It is only hearsay, something we are told and which we may accept on faith. The important fact is that this Buddha nature does not illuminate and transform our ordinary lives. It is somewhat like having talent for music. We may be told we have this talent, and the knowledge may be gratifying, but we are still unable to play the piano. The potential is there, and the potential is a reality, but we still are unable to activate and realize the buried talent. If the individual begins to practice, the talent itself will become evident in the practice. The very ability to play the piano is itself this latent talent now realized in actuality. But if the talented person does not begin to practice, he might as well not have the ability at all. Our Buddha nature is like this. "To disport oneself freely in this [jijuyu] samadhi, the right entrance is proper sitting in zazen. This Dharma is amply present in every person, but unless one practices, it is not manifested, unless there is realization, it is not attained."[3]

Dōgen Zenji himself speaks often of "realization," and the Japanese word which is translated as "realization" literally means "proof", "evidence", "certification", and "witnessing". *satori* All these words carry the sense of authenticating and bringing out into the open. The English word "realization" literally means "making real", which is close to the meaning of the Japanese term. Realization of Buddha nature therefore ✓ means making real what otherwise is only an interesting rumor. The whole point of Buddhism as an experiential religion is this real-making process whereby Buddha nature becomes a concrete, lived reality.

Therefore, because practice is absolutely necessary for making our inherent Buddha nature a lived reality, there is no end to practice. As long as we imagine that practice is only a self-serving means to a greater end, practice will be undertaken in the spirit of a person who invests in the stock market in order to reap greater profits eventually. Also, when practice is conceived of in this manner, there will be the tendency to think that once one has acquired some small insight, practice is no longer necessary. But if the truth is that we are each a ✓ complete Buddha with the totality of Buddha vision, then there can never be an end to the realization of this nature, for there is no limit to its ability to encompass more and more of experience. There is indeed a real question of whether a person who desires enlightenment so ardently can ever acquire it, since by definition Buddhahood is complete desirelessness. In fact, Dōgen Zenji says that all that is required is simple faith in one's intrinsic Buddha nature.[4] In *Shōji* ("Birth and Death") he says:

You only attain the mind of buddha when there is no hating [of birth and death] and no desiring [of nirvana]. But do not try to gauge it with your mind or speak it with words. When you simply release and forget both your body and mind and throw yourself into the house of buddha, and when functioning comes from the direction of buddha and you go in accord with it, then with no strength needed and no thought expended, freed from birth and death, you become buddha. Then there can be no obstacle in any man's mind. There is an extremely easy way to become buddha. Refraining from all evils, not clinging to birth and death, working in deep compassion for all sentient beings, respecting those over you and pitying those below you, without any detesting or desiring, worrying or lamentation—this is what is called buddha. Do not search beyond it.[5]

This faith in one's intrinsic Buddha nature is none other than the life of endless practice. To "throw ourselves into the house of the Buddha" is to have deep faith in the reality of this nature, and practice is simply allowing this nature to actualize or "realize" itself in our daily lives. It is practice forever. From time to time there may be flashes of *satori* insight, sometimes grand and overwhelming, sometimes small and modest, but practice goes on and on. The master may test the depth of our insight from time to time by means of judiciously chosen *kōans*, and he may certify our understanding, but the practice continues. "When Buddhas are truly Buddhas," says Dōgen, "there is no need to know that we are all Buddhas, but we are realized Buddhas and further advance in realizing Buddha."[6] If, like Methuselah in the Hebrew scriptures, we were able to live for 900 years, we would continue to practice and continue to realize the Buddha we are. The horizons of Buddha vision are boundless and limitless, and the depths to which it can penetrate are fathomless.

This practice is very simple, but it is also very difficult. It is our human nature to pick and choose, to desire and loathe, to form a myriad attitudes and judgements towards the events of our lives. This practice is difficult because it demands of us that we simply cease the picking and choosing, desiring and loathing. A contemporary Zen master has said that "Zen is picking up your coat from the floor and hanging it up." That is all that is required, and nothing could be simpler. Yet how difficult! There is no fun in "picking up your coat," and all such tasks are not at all self-fulfilling and enriching. They do not make us richer, or more powerful, or sexier, or more personable. How much more rewarding and fun it is just to read another book on self-improvement, or spend the day at the beach, watch television, go to a party, take a course in self-assertiveness, or join a protest demonstration for the latest cause. Worse, however, is the fact that "picking up your coat" doesn't seem to be a very "spiritual" kind of practice, like prayer, meditation, fasting, or developing a meaningful relationship. There is nothing more ordinary and unspecial than "picking up your coat." Yet, it is really the essence of practice, for "picking up your coat" is exactly what Dōgen means by meditation.

Just what practice encompasses is the subject of the remaining parts of this book. But here I would like to begin to clarify what I mean when I say that "picking up your coat" is the essence of practice. It is particularly important for Western people to understand this, because we have all been raised in a culture where it is usually assumed that religious activities are of a special nature; indeed, religion itself is felt to be a sphere apart from the mundane world. The statement that religious practice—meditation—consists of "picking up your coat" may seem absurd at first glance, because we almost always pick up the coat, or wash the dishes, or perform any other task of that sort with regret or dislike. We imagine that there are alternative activities which are more valuable, or more rewarding, or more pleasing. While we pick up the clothes from the floor, we yearn to be elsewhere, doing better things. We are bored, impatient, and even somewhat resentful. Of course, doing things in this manner is not Zen at all, because our minds are filled with likes and dislikes. But the rest of our lives are going to be made up of countless situations of this kind, and the question is whether we will continue to approach them with irritation and regret, hoping for better things elsewhere, later, or whether we will begin to see this ordinary life as Buddha sees it. Perhaps our ordinary life will in time come to seem good enough, even beautiful, to us. It is important to begin to practice.

Unfortunately, most choose not to practice. Non-practice means continuing to approach every situation with self-centered attitudes. "Is it going to benefit me?" we ask, or "Is it a threat to me?" All about us we see things which we imagine are "good" or "bad", but these goods and bads are only good and bad for me, for that is what "good" and "bad" mean for most of us. This hierarchy of self-oriented values becomes more complex and deep-rooted the older we become, and it is just this mesh of attitudes and valuations which obscure our Buddha nature. To restore, or realize, our Buddha nature, we need to remove this mesh and come to see that dishwashing is not really "bad" and becoming chairman of the board of directors is not really "good", for the good and bad we constantly perceive about us are nothing more than reflections of our self-concern. Dōgen's zazen, the jijiyu samadhi, is a way to eliminate this obscuring veil, for by its very nature it is the experience of events without subjective judgements. But it is not a preparation for the sake of a future realization; in jijiyu samadhi we begin to realize the Buddha we are right here and now. As we live this samadhi we live the life of Buddha, for in it we are empty, which is being Buddha.

Ideally, and hopefully, this samadhi comes to be our

12

everyday consciousness, wherever we are, at all times. It is not a special consciousness reserved for the meditation room for an hour in the morning and evening. Nor does it mean to go about in a dreamy, semi-wakeful state, as if we were anesthetized or drugged. In samadhi we know pain as pain and pleasure as pleasure; the alert and receptive mind reflects all events clearly and without distortion. The only difference is that we do not correlate the experience with some idea, mainly "good" or "bad". It means to live the experience one hundred per cent, without adding to it any subjective judgement. The difficulty lies in this not adding to the experience.

Hui-neng defines this zazen practice in the following way:

> What is it in this teaching we call "sitting in meditation"(*tso-ch'an*)? In this teaching, "sitting" means without any obstruction anywhere, outwardly and under all circumstances, not to activate thoughts. "Meditation" is internally to see the original nature and not become confused.[7]

= zazen?

To "sit", then, means to stop correlating external events with ideas such as "it is this", or "it is that", "right", "wrong", and so on, ad infinitum. It has nothing to do with anesthesia or with escaping anything, for when the snow falls, we will still shiver and get our hair wet, when the pangs of disease strike, we will suffer the pain, and when the voracious tiger of old age springs, we will be devoured like anyone else. Dōgen says that the secret is not hating these things and not desiring their alternatives; it means to realize that there are really only these things and nothing else. When the great Chinese Zen master Ta-mei was dying, his students asked him for a final helpful word. "When it comes, don't try to avoid it; when it goes, don't go running after it," said Ta-mei. Just then, a squirrel chattered on the roof. "There is only this, there is nothing else," he said, and then he died. Can we conceive of what "this" is? Can "this" be enough for us? Is there another reality more real or more wonderful than "this"? To know that there is only "this" is to "see the original nature and not become confused."

The key to practice is the development of this samadhi and its retention in all activities. Daily formal sitting in zazen will establish a model for this samadhi which we can in time learn to retain and use to illuminate our ordinary life. When we "pick up the coat" as a Buddha activity, two things occur. First, it is no longer a profane and lowly act but the functioning of Buddha nature. Second, it is ceaseless training through which this Buddha activity comes to grow and include more and more within its scope. Because there are no limits to the amount of experience that can be illuminated by this activity, there is also no end to practice.

So this practice is simple, but it is difficult. The difficulty lies in not adding something extra to the events of our life. The practice I have been discussing might also be called the practice of the art of doing just one thing at a time. It is wonderful to learn to do one thing at a time. When we do formal zazen, we just sit; this means we do not add to the sitting any judgements such as how wonderful it is to do zazen, or how badly we are doing, or "When will I become a Buddha?". We just sit. When we wash the dishes, we just wash dishes, when we drive on the highway, we just drive. When pain comes, there is just pain, and when pleasure comes, there is just pleasure. There is nothing more to do than to learn to do one thing at a time. A Buddha is someone who is totally at one with his experience at every moment.

Dōgen's Zen is the Zen of practice. There is really no big graduation day when the training stops, because we are already that which we seek, and practice is learning day-by-day to be what we are. The starting point is intrinsic Buddhahood. Real meditation is the alert, clear-minded attention to the details of daily life when we "do not activate thoughts" towards these activities. To do this even to some slight extent is to realize one's Buddha nature to that extent, and the necessity of realizing this nature fully commits us to practice forever. This is what it means to follow Dōgen's Way.

Practice must therefore include all activities. Obviously practice cannot be limited to the formal activities of the zendō, when we chant, bow, offer incense, and do zazen. Real zazen must begin when we open our eyes in the morning and end when we close them at night, so that all the intervening activities of the day become practice. There sometimes seems to be the feeling that many, or most, of these other activities are not practice, however. Earning money with which to eat, maintaining the buildings and grounds where we practice and live, fund raising, keeping our living quarters neat and clean, treating food and clothing with respect and gratitude, following the many regulations imposed on a community of people working and practicing together—these are often thought of as distractions from practice, nuisances, or at best necessary evils which support real practice. Dōgen realized that it is comparatively easy to think that one wants to practice, to seek out a teacher, and to enter the activities of the meditation hall, but it is difficult to do all the other things which we do not associate with practice. "Entering the deep mountains and thinking about the Buddha Way is comparatively easy, while building stupas and making Buddha images is very difficult," he says. They are difficult because unless a person has a very real commitment to following the Way and understands this commitment as a total response to all events and activities, these ordinary activities will be a real burden. Learning the Way must therefore include niceties of etiquette between individuals who practice together, for this is nothing more than respect for their Buddha nature. Many activities are ideally gestures of respect towards the Buddha, his Dharma, and the community of training individuals, and without this respect, there can be no progress in the Way. Many things that need to be done are not for ourselves but for our successors, like Lin-chi planting cedars for those who would come after him. The Mahayana emphasis on helping all living beings thus includes not only those living now but also those who will come after us. All these activities become practice for the person who has what Dōgen called "the mind which seeks the Way." When one has dropped off mind and body and no longer hankers for fame and profit, when one has become as empty as the minds of the birds that sing in the trees, when one is truly grateful to the Buddha and his descendents, then all activities become practice. When there is no distinction of sacred and profane, profitable and non-profitable, practice and nonpractice, then every gesture is practice in learning the Way. It is learning to raise an ox.

The most impressive aspect of Dōgen's Way is the insistence on utter seriousness and utter commitment. It is inspiring, and somewhat disheartening, to read the *Zuimonki*, *Gakudō yōjinshū*, or the essays translated in this volume, for Dōgen tolerates no half-hearted, self-serving, or dilettantish involvement in the Way. One must pursue the Way in the single-minded and earnest manner of a person trying to extinguish a fire in his hair. Anything less than this is only a waste of the individual's time, for he will never succeed unless learning the Way is the most important thing in his life. How can anyone hope to measure up to Dōgen's terribly demanding requirements? Practice is a very serious matter, one that demands full effort at all times. To read the various chapters on practice in the *Shōbōgenzō* is to become aware of what a rare person Dōgen Zenji was, and why there is no grander conception of the religious life to be found anywhere.

The ten chapters I have translated are all about this practice. Philosophy is not entirely absent, but for the most part they are about practice, specifically the various forms that practice takes. I have chosen these ten chapters because they are representative of the various dimensions of practice, because they are powerful and beautiful in their spirit and rhetorical force, because they exhibit so well Dōgen's stern and uncompromising spirit, and because I find them so moving and convincing. There are surely other chapters of *Shōbōgenzō* which could have been included. For instance, any collection ought to include *Genjō kōan*, which is pertinent to practice and is surely one of the most brilliant, profound, and moving religious documents in world religious literature. I have not included it because it has already been well translated by others, and I cannot improve on these translations.[8] Also, I might have included a chapter on atonement, which, perhaps surprisingly, is important in Dōgen's ideas about practice. In fact, it is hoped that in the near future, all of *Shōbōgenzō* will be translated accurately so that Western people will have easy access to one of the glittering jewels of world religious and philosophical literature.

The following expository chapters are included here in the earnest hope that they will help to clarify just what Dōgen Zenji means by practice. Just what the essence of that practice is, is beyond my powers to express in a word or two. Dōgen uses several expressions to indicate the same thing. Therefore, any one of these expressions is adequate, provided we understand that all the other alternative expressions mean the same thing. Therefore, we might say that the essence of practice is *shinjin datsuraku*, which means "mind and body dropped off." It is synonymous with "emptiness", and denotes a state in which one is no longer motivated by self-concern. But it seems clear from the essays translated here that, in a very real way, *shinjin datsuraku* is the same as *shukke*, which means "home departure". Consequently, to really leave home, or the world, is the same as dropping off mind and body. However, again, both terms can be seen as identical with *hotsu mujō shin*, "arousing the supreme thought," or "arousing the determination to attain the supreme." Practice, or continuous practice (*gyōji*), which I have been discussing above, is none other than the whole of daily activity performed by one who embodies these things. The essence of practice is enunciated clearly in all the chapters of *Shōbōgenzō* translated here. They allow us to obtain some idea of what it is that Dōgen's Way requires. Nothing less will do.

## NOTES

1. *The Platform Sutra of the Sixth Patriarch*, trans. Philip B. Yampolsky (New York: Columbia University Press, 1967), p. 135.

2. *Bendōwa*, trans. Norman Waddell and Abe Masao, in *Eastern Buddhist*, 6, no. 1 (1973), p. 128.

3. *Ibid.*, p. 129.

4. *Bendōwa*, in *Dōgen shū (Nihon no shisō*, Vol. 2), ed. Tamaki Koshirō (Tokyo: Chikuma Shobo, 1969), p. 130.

5. *Shōji*, trans. Norman Waddell and Abe Masao, in *Eastern Buddhist*, 5, no. 1 (1972), pp. 79–80.

6. *Genjō kōan*, trans. Taizan Maezumi Roshi and Francis Cook (Los Angeles: Zen Center of Los Angeles Press, 1977), p. 2. This is a revision of the translation by Chōtan Aitken Roshi and Tanahashi Kazuaki.

7. *The Platform Sutra of the Sixth Patriarch*, p. 140.

8. *Genjō kōan.* See note 6 above.

# TWO

*The Importance of Faith*

Practice is not possible without faith. It may be startling to hear that faith is important in Zen, but the fact is that it has always been an important part of Buddhism throughout its twenty-five-hundred-year history. This is because of the nature of Buddhism as a religion. Prior to the experiential realization of the truth of the Buddha's teachings, one must proceed in practice in the faith that the teachings are true and that practice will culminate in enlightenment. Without this faith, there is no support for the practice, and if there is doubt or lack of assurance, one will either not begin practice or else will not continue it once it has started. In all of Buddhism prior to the arising of the Zen tradition, faith has thus had a crucial function in the life of the meditator. Many of the lists of practices, mental states, and stages of development of the early abhidharma literature include *shraddhā* (faith) as one of the items. When the meditator begins to verify the teachings of Buddhism in his own experience, faith is no longer re-

19

quired, for it is now replaced with knowledge. This differs from the Christian tradition, for instance, where faith is so important that it ranks even above obedience to God's will and remains the central way of being religious throughout the life of the believer. There is not, in other words, a time for the Christian when faith is no longer important, for the tenets of his religion are never experientially validated in the way the doctrines of Buddhism are. In Buddhism, on the other hand, it is always the first phase of development, and while it is necessary, it is something to be dropped away eventually. There is, for the Buddhist, therefore, a vast difference between believing that all things are impermanent, for instance, and knowing that they are, but before this becomes knowledge, one must practice in the faith that it is so and will eventually be proven to be so.

Before going on, it might be well to define Buddhist faith. We can begin by enumerating the kinds of faith it is not. First of all, faith may be nothing more than the intellectual acceptance of a doctrine or creed. In this case, faith amounts to an act of the will, whereby the individual feels that he *ought* to accept such-and-such a teaching. I may be taught that a supernatural being exists, and in order to qualify as an orthodox member of a community, I will agree that this is the case, even though there is no real reason for doing so. In fact, many people profess belief in a god, resurrection of the body, and final judgement, but the merely intellectual acceptance of the ideas is evident from the fact that their lives do not correspond to the belief. Second, faith may take the form of passionate, blind acceptance of an idea which can never really be validated because of the nature of the teaching. Consequently, though I will never in this life know (in the strict sense of knowing) if personal immortality is a fact, I may cling tenaciously to the idea and organize my life in accordance with the idea. Third, faith may approach a kind of certainty, because the object of faith is a common, recurrent phenomenon in one's life and therefore deserves the faith.

For instance, I can have faith in the arising of the sun tomorrow morning because it has in fact risen every morning of my life so far, and though there is always a chance that it may not rise tomorrow morning, I can be reasonably justified in my faith. This is an easy kind of faith because I can rely on past experience.

None of the above examples closely resembles Buddhist faith. Buddhist faith is a very deep certitude in the veracity of a certain doctrine, accepted and used as a touchstone for conduct in the faith that practice will verify its truth. The object of faith may be an idea, one's teacher, or the trustworthiness of the Buddha himself, but in any case, there is a complete certainty that one is confronting something on which one may totally rely. The object of faith may be trusted provisionally because Buddhism itself teaches that the faith will eventually be replaced by knowledge and that any teaching not verifiable in this way ought to be rejected. Consequently, such faith is not blind and irrational, nor is it a mere intellectual adherence to creedal orthodoxy. The acceptance is provisional because of the necessity of eventually replacing the faith with knowledge, but even in its provisional status, the faith amounts to a kind of certainty because of the anticipation of validation. The faith is further strengthened because of one's association with people who actualize this knowledge in their lives. And because Buddhism as a religion is based on each individual's realization of the Buddha's own enlightenment, ideally, there can never be a question of reliance on faith alone throughout life.

The various chapters of *Shōbōgenzō* show that there are several objects of faith, but in the last analysis, all are the same. One has faith in the Buddha. One must have faith in one's teacher, but is he not a surrogate Buddha inasmuch as he has inherited the Buddha's mind from his own teacher, and so on back to the time of Śākyamuni himself? This is the meaning of the patriarchal succession. One must also have faith in the teachings of Buddhism, but are these not merely verbal expressions of the Buddha mind? Also, and most important of all, one must have faith in one's own intrinsic Buddha nature, for Zen teaches that all things are the Buddha. It is no exaggeration to say that this faith is the very door through which one enters the Dharma. Dōgen Zenji therefore says, "The Buddha once said, 'The person who is without faith is like a broken jug'. This means that living beings who do not have faith in the Buddha's teaching cannot be vessels of the teaching. The Buddha also said, 'The great ocean of the Buddha's teaching is entered through the door of faith'. Clearly know that those beings who have no faith are those people who do not dwell in it."[1]

Thus, faith is the entry way to the Dharma, but at the same time, correct practice is based on the faith that one is already a Buddha, for there is nothing that is not the Buddha. "Grass, trees, all are [Buddha] mind and body," says Dōgen in *Hotsu mujō shin*. "If the myriad dharmas are not born, neither is the One Mind born. If all dharmas are marked with this ultimate reality, then [even] a speck of dust is marked with it. The One Mind is all dharmas; all dharmas are the One Mind, the whole body [of the Buddha]."[2] Consequently, unless practice is undertaken in the faith that oneself is the Buddha, and that everything else, even a speck of dust, is also the Buddha and preaches the Dharma with a clear voice, realization of the fact will be impossible.

Dōgen did not compose a separate chapter on faith in *Shōbōgenzō*, but there are many scattered statements about it in various chapters which leave no doubt that it is the basis for practice. For instance, in *Gakudō yōjinshū* (which is not part of *Shōbōgenzō*), he says,

> Practicing the Way of the Buddha means you must have faith in the Buddha Way. Having faith in the Buddha Way means you first must have faith that you originally abide in the Way, are not deluded, are not mistaken, neither gain nor lose [in Buddha wisdom],

and are not in error. If you arouse this kind
of faith, illuminate the Way in this manner,
and rely on it and practice it, it is the basis for
enlightenment.[3]

It is not only the basis for practice and the entry into the
Dharma, faith is none other than practice itself.

Zazen, for instance, is surely the main practice in Dōgen's
Zen, but practice takes other forms also, as I have already
indicated in the first chapter. Home departure *(shukke)* is
practice, as is receiving and maintaining the precepts *(jukai)*,
venerating all the Buddhas, taking the threefold refuge *(kie
sambō)*, wearing the robes of a monk, repenting one's bad
deeds *(karma)*, making images and reliquary containers
*(stūpas)*, asking questions of the master, and others. It is interesting that Dōgen interprets all these forms of practice as
expressions of faith. For instance, atonement, which Dōgen
says is the examination of one's own wicked behavior, is not
just an oral confession and a decision not to do evil again, but
in essence consists of a firm faith and dedicated practice. To
have faith in the Buddha and his teaching and to commit
oneself without reservation to hard practice is atonement.[4]
Taking refuge in the Three Treasures means relying completely on Buddha, Dharma, and Sangha, and not on one's
own abilities, so that really, taking refuge in them is a statement of faith in their reality and power. In *Kie sambō* ("Taking
Refuge in the Three Treasures"), Dōgen says,

> With regard to taking refuge in the Three
> Treasures, with pure faith in your abdomen,
> whether the *Tathāgata* dwells in the world
> or does not, join the palms of your hands
> together, bow your head, and say, "I, so-and-
> so, from now on until I become a Buddha,
> take refuge in the Buddha, I take refuge in
> his teaching, I take refuge in the community
> of followers, etc."[5]

Dōgen's attitude towards the monk's robe *(kesa)* is also instructive. The kesa is not simply a distinguishing costume, nor is it just clothing worn by a specific group of people. It is to be treated with great respect, no matter how old and tattered it may become, because it is symbolic of, and an embodiment of, the Dharma itself. Thus, to take the precepts and wear the kesa is to acknowledge faith in the Dharma and to wear the Dharma on one's body.

> It is clear that the Dharma which is symbolized by the kesa has been transmitted from master to master. To think that it is without value or that it has not been correctly transmitted is evidence of lack of faith. He who is interested in arousing the thought of enlightenment must be instructed in the correct transmission of the patriarchs. He is then not only a person who has encountered the Dharma, which is hard to encounter, he is in fact a descendent of the Dharma which is correctly transmitted in the form of the Buddha's robe. He sees it, learns it, and now wears the robe. In other words, he is in reality standing right in front of the Buddha, meeting him, hearing him preach the Dharma, and being illuminated by his light. [Wearing the kesa] means using what the Buddha used and transmitting the Buddha's mind to oneself. It means acquiring the essence of the Buddha.[6]

The object of faith in this passage is twofold: one is the Dharma itself as taught by the Buddha, the other is the Zen master as one who has inherited this Dharma in the patriarchal succession. The kesa which one wears is the visible Dharma, and wearing it expresses one's faith.

The merits of the kesa enable us to realize the truth

within ourselves. "The kesa correctly transmits the skin, flesh, bones, and marrow of Śākyamuni, the Blessed One. . . . Those who receive the kesa, wear it, and hold it reverently to their heads will without doubt become enlightened in two or three lifetimes."[7] Thus to put on the kesa is the same as putting on the Dharma, as the "Kesa Verse" says:

> How wonderful is the robe of liberation,
> A markless field of merit.
> I place the Buddha's teaching on my body,
> And liberate living beings everywhere.[8]

It seems clear from these passages, as well as many others not included here, that faith is the indispensable basis for practice. In *Bendōwa*, Dōgen says,

> The realm of Buddhas is inconceivable and beyond the reach of the intellect. How can it be reached by someone who has no faith, who has little knowledge? Only a person with a great motive can attain it. For the person who is lacking in faith, it is impossible. When right faith arises in the mind, one should practice and study under a master.[9]

Certainly, faith is important, but I would like to express the truth of the matter in an even stronger way: Dōgen's Zen is the Zen of faith. That is, it is a religion in which faith is the very mechamism whereby the goal is achieved, and in the absence of which the door to the truth remains closed. It is therefore not simply one important element among others; it is the indispensable prerequisite.

Japanese and Chinese Buddhists have for centuries distinguished the various forms of Buddhism by means of a system called (in Japanese) *kyōhan*, "doctrinal classification." In this system, a dominant characteristic of each form of Buddhism is isolated and used to distinguish between that form and all other forms. Every form of Buddhism classifies in this way. For example, the Pure Land Buddhism of Shinran has always referred to itself as the "way of faith," while all other forms, including Zen, are referred to as the "saintly way." The "saintly way" refers to practices which presumably involve meditation, concern with moral purification, learning, and the like. It has also been said that Pure Land Buddhism is the way of the "other power," while Zen and other forms of Buddhism are the "way of self power." The reason for this is that in Pure Land Buddhism, the way is through complete dependence on the saving power of another, the Buddha Amida, while Zen practitioners depend on their own efforts to achieve emancipation. Faith is therefore considered important in Pure Land Buddhism but not nearly so important in Zen. However, it may be asked whether this is an accurate characterization of Zen and whether it is true to the facts in general. Several Japanese scholars, including Akiyama Hanji and Okada Gihō, have claimed as I do that Dōgen's Zen is a Buddhism of faith.[10] Since I feel that this interpretation is an accurate one, I would like to give some reasons why I think faith is important in Dōgen's Zen.

One way to make sense of the bewildering proliferation of Buddhist schools, doctrines, and practices over the last 2,500 years is to see them as a single, creative, ongoing effort to deal with the central problem of Buddhism, which is the erroneous belief in an enduring, permanent self. Whether it is Zen, Pure Land, Theravada, or Tibetan Buddhist practice, it is always practice which will effectively destroy the belief in this self. Dōgen's Zen, with its stress on faith, is no different; that is, the mechanism of faith is effective in dealing with the problem of the self. The necessity of *shinjin datsuraku*, "the dropping off of body and mind," is the necessity of understanding that oneself, and all others, are empty of this self which is only a convenient fiction. But the question is, How does one drop off body and mind? How does one achieve emptiness?

It seems that there have been primarily two different

ways of achieving this result in the history of world Buddhism. The way of pre-Mahayana Buddhism and the Theravada Buddhism of present day Southeast Asia and Ceylon has been the way of frontal assault. This is the method of *śamatha* and *vipaśyanā* meditations, which first put obstructive emotions and impulses asleep in *śamatha* exercises, then subject the self to the corrosive analysis of *vipaśyanā* insight practices. The final achievement is the destruction of the illusory self. The other method, which is generally Mahayana and takes various forms, is an indirect method. It is indirect because instead of attacking the idea of a self directly, the illusion is destroyed in the process of directing one's will and attention in another direction. For instance, the Mahayana emphasis on compassion and the bodhisattva's career of selfless service in behalf of others accomplishes this by gradually diminishing self-serving, self-interested action. The saying "to help others is to help oneself" means that in the process of devoting oneself unconditionally to helping all living beings, one becomes more and more capable of acting in a non-self-serving manner. I would like to suggest that faith accomplishes the same goal in Dōgen's Zen. And, of course, because this Zen is Mahayana Buddhism, there is the same bodhisattva vow, so that the individual involved in this Zen practice is working towards the goal in the traditional Mahayana fashion. The approach must be indirect for the reasons mentioned earlier: the direct pursuit of enlightenment is a confession of dualistic thinking and merely one more attempt to seek self-gratification, and both of these are self-defeating.

It is for this reason that Dōgen Zenji so often warns against any kind of seeking or wanting, even if the object of the desire is a "holy" object. "If you wish to practice the Way of the Buddhas and patriarchs, you should follow without thought of profit the Way of the former sages and the conduct of the patriarchs, expecting nothing, seeking nothing, and gaining nothing. Cut off the mind that seeks and do not cherish a desire to gain the fruits of Buddhahood," he says in the *Zuimonki*.[11] But how does one practice if one should not think of practicing *for* something? As I have already said, there are several ways of doing this in Mahayana Buddhism. One method, which I will speak of more in detail in the next chapter, is that of making a vow to emancipate all living beings even though oneself is not completely emancipated, which is the traditional bodhisattva vow. By doing practice in this manner, even though one has an objective, which is to emancipate all living beings, it is not a self-gratifying objective. The other method is to commit oneself utterly to practicing the Way, but in the understanding that it is not oneself who is carrying out the practice. Thus, when one sits in formal zazen, it is not the self, individual "X", who sits, but the Buddha who sits in zazen. The gradual clarification of one's experience as a result of zazen is not the result of the individual's clarifying and spiritualizing his own mind, but is the Buddha being a Buddha; that is, it is the Buddha who is realizing Buddhahood, as Dōgen says. And this begins to happen when we completely abandon our own efforts and trust completely in our true nature which is the Buddha. This is where faith comes in.

The point to what has been written above is this: faith is important in Dōgen's Zen because practice must be undertaken in the trust in another—the Buddha—to realize itself in and through us, which means that there must be faith in the other as the necessary basis of practice. Consequently, Dōgen's Zen is not really the Buddhism of self power *(jiriki)*, as Pure Land Buddhists say, it is the Buddhism of other power *(tariki)*. One may indeed practice the Buddhism of self power, and many do, but it will not be Dōgen's way. It is my feeling that Dōgen's approach to practice and realization is the culmination of Buddhism's historical attempt to deal with the problem of the self and its actions, and is thus the most sophisticated and profound solution to the problem.

In Shinran's Pure Land Buddhism, it is taught that libera-

tion and final nirvana are gifts given by Amida and not goods
which are acquired by our own efforts. In fact, in order for
Amida's wonderful gift to become a reality for us, we must
not try to gain them by our own efforts. In a time countless
cosmic eons in the past, when Amida was still a practicing
bodhisattva named Dharmākara, he made a number of vows,
the essence of which was that he, Dharmākara, would never
enter into the state of final, complete Buddhahood until and
unless every other living being also achieved the same Buddhahood. Through countless, inconceivable practices he accumulated a vast store of merit and finally did become the
Buddha Amida. What this means is that in some sense, all
living beings are guaranteed Buddhahood, and therefore
also, in some sense, are already Buddhas, because the condition of the vows was that Dharmākara would not become a
Buddha unless every other living being did also. The fact of
his present Buddhahood implies the present Buddhahood of
all beings. In other words, the conditions of the vow are
fulfilled. Once an individual becomes aware of what Amida
has done for him, that is, once faith in the vows has arisen in
his heart, he is then reborn in Amida's paradise when he dies,
where he will speedily achieve enlightenment. The key to
rebirth in the Western Paradise of Amida is faith in the vows,
faith amounting to an unshakable conviction.

Faith in the vows of Amida is faith in the fact that the
causal practices which culminate in rebirth in the Pure Land
are Amida's practices and not one's own. It is therefore also
faith in the fact that all that needs to be done for rebirth in the
Pure Land has already been done, and done by the Buddha.
This faith arises once the sinful individual realizes that his
own puny efforts are insufficient to cause this rebirth, and in
total passive surrender turns to Amida. But it is not only that
he realizes that he *can* not help the process; he *must* not try to
help, for any efforts on his own part are a tacit admission of
doubt in Amida's vows and at the same time an egoistic confidence in his own goodness and abilities. There is only one

way to turn, and that is towards Amida, in complete faith in Amida's compassionate gift to him. The arising of faith is itself nothing other than the actualization of Amida's vow within him.

When we look deeper into this matter of faith and try to determine what is actually happening in the life of the believer, it becomes evident that faith exactly coincides with the complete abandonment of self-effort and a turning to Amida, for as was pointed out above, self-effort is itself an admission of doubt in the power of Amida's vows. As Daisetz Suzuki and others have noted, if we strip away the mythological trappings of the situation, we find that what is spoken of as a kind of knowledge that one has really been saved by Amida is a form of satori, and this satori occurs when, and only when, the individual ceases to rely on his own power and ability. Is this not the forgetting of the self which Dōgen speaks of in *Genjō kōan*? Is there a more powerful form of this self-forgetting than abandoning oneself completely to the Other?

What I am saying, then, is that the reason why faith is necessary, and why it is so powerful, is that in turning completely to the Other, we begin to forget the self and its incessant demands. It might be said that the human tendency to seek self-gratification through self-reliance begins to diminish in inverse ratio to our faith and trust in our inherent Buddha nature and its ability to actualize itself. Thus, Dōgen tells us to throw ourselves into the house of the Buddha. A young Sōtō Zen monk once remarked, "We can find complete freedom and tranquility in ourselves when we have left ourselves completely to the Buddha's boundlessly wide mind."[12] Dōgen knew this from his own experience, and therefore his life was spent teaching a Buddhism of faith in the power of the Other, who is the Buddha.

It is difficult to overstate the matter. To have faith in the Buddha is the same as forgetting the self. How can it be otherwise when the prime requirement for "learning the Way" is to forget the self, *shinjin datsuraku*? The dropping off of one's own body and mind and the minds and bodies of others is the almost incredible and inconceivable act of becoming totally empty, whereby we are no longer attached to anything (even nirvana), in which there is nothing to desire, nothing to expect, nothing to be. The vexing dualisms of life are transcended and all discriminations cease to operate. But how does one achieve this life if practice itself is a greater attachment, and if one's practice is based on dualisms even more absolute than the ordinary ones? It is like trying to fight fire with fire, an even greater entanglement in contradictions and confusion.

It may be useful to think of faith as a form of humility. Humility is a realistic appraisal of one's status and ability in the face of greater value and ability. To be humble is to approach experience without the attitude that one is the center of the universe. Its opposite is pride, which the ancient Greeks portrayed in their drama as the most destructive force in the lives of both the protagonist and those about him. But pride cannot coexist with the certainty that there is something else of greater power, beauty, and ability, a something which trivializes one's own values, motives, and abilities.

Faith, then, is the faith in the reality and power of this other, and practice is practice which allows this deeper mind to illuminate our experience. In the final analysis, there is really no difference between this faith and zazen itself. The definition of zazen in the first chapter was that "sitting" means not activating thoughts towards external events, and "zen" means seeing one's true nature and not being confused. True zazen, then, is any activity carried out without self-concern, not forming self-serving attitudes towards events, and living one's ordinary life without attachment or loathing. It is the same as forgetting the self. To forget this self is nothing more than to have faith in the ability of the Buddha to illuminate our lives with Buddha insight. Nothing more is required. Thus, Dōgen Zenji says:

When I see an ignorant old monk sitting
wordlessly, I think of the story of the woman
with faith who became enlightened by giving a feast. It does not depend on knowledge, books, words, or long explanations. It
just requires the aid of true faith.[13]

# NOTES

1. Quoted by Akiyama Hanji in *Dōgen no kenkyū* (Tokyo: Reimei
Shobo, 1965), p. 248.

2. From *Hotsu mujō shin,* in Okada Gihō, *Shōbōgenzō shisō Taikei*
(Tokyo: Hosei University Press, 1954), Vol. 6, p. 77.

3. From *Gakudō yōjinshū,* quoted by Yamaguchi Shinju, in "Dōgen
Zenji ni okeru shingyō no Mondai," *Indogaku bukkyōgaku kenkyū,* 13, No. 1
(1965), p. 83.

4. *Shōbōgenzō shisō taikei,* Vol. 6, p. 15.

5. *Kie sambō. Shōbōgenzō shisō taikei,* Vol. 6, p. 176.

6. *Kesa kudoku. Dōgen shū (Nihon no shisō,* Vol. 2), ed. Tamaki
Koshirō (Tokyo: Chikuma Shobo, 1969), pp. 270–71.

7. *Ibid.,* p. 276.

8. *Ibid.,* p. 289. This is recited daily in the *zendō.*

9. *Bendōwa,* in *Dōgen shū,* p. 104.

10. Akiyama, *Dōgen no kenkyū,* p. 325 and Okada, *Shōbōgenzō shisō
taikei,* Vol. 6, p. 17.

11. Masunaga Reihō, tarns., *Zuimonki* (Honolulu: East-West Center
Press, 1971), p. 56.

12. Karako Shojo, "My Faith in Shikan-taza," unpublished type-
script, n.d.

13. *Bendōwa,* in *Dōgen shū,* p. 130.

# THREE

*Arousing the Thought of Enlightenment*

It is easy to merely play the game formally in a discipline such as Zen. It is pleasant and rewarding to wear meditation robes, chant the sutras and mantras, bow to the Buddha, and sit in zazen. Anyone who has done much chanting knows that it gives one a feeling of euphoria, and one may think that this good feeling is spiritual or that it indicates growth. Activities such as chanting, bowing, and sitting in zazen are not at all wasted, even when done merely formally, for even this superficial encounter with the Dharma will have some wholesome outcome at a later time. However, it must be said in the most unambiguous terms that this is not real Zen. To follow the Dharma involves a complete reorientation of one's life in such a way that one's activities are manifestations of, and are filled with, a deeper meaning. If it were not otherwise, and merely sitting in zazen were enough, every frog in the pond would be enlightened, as one Zen master said. Dōgen Zenji himself said that one must practice Zen with the attitude of a person trying to extinguish a fire in his hair. That is, Zen must be practiced with an attitude of single-minded urgency.

Zen therefore must be the dominant concern in one's life to which all other considerations are subordinated. Otherwise, the merely formal observance of Zen customs is a waste of a person's life. Thus, one turns away from ordinary things and turns to Zen as the most important thing in one's life. By "turning away," I do not mean a literal cessation of ordinary activities, but rather a change in attitude towards them. This kind of turning away is a reordering of values, really, because now, instead of seeking ultimate fulfillment and goodness in pleasure, power, wealth, or a fine reputation, one seeks the Dharma as having the greatest value and the greatest potential for fulfillment. As I will explain in a later chapter, this reorientation of values is also called "home departure" *(shukke)*, but here I wish to discuss it in terms of a sincere, profound determination to follow the Dharma. The traditional term for this is "arousing the thought of enlightenment" (Sanskrit: *bodhicittotpāda*; Japanese: *hotsu bodai shin*).

This new determination to follow the Dharma is not a simple matter of coolly deciding that one is going to start meditating and living a more "spiritual" life. Decisions of this sort are very easily rescinded, because we have not yet realized that the goods which most people treasure cannot really bring us happiness and contentment. This determination is, on the one hand, a kind of conversion which is very deep and moving, because it signals a profound disillusionment with life as it is lived by most people. It comes with the realization that real contentment and goodness do not come from sensual self-gratification, controlling the destinies of other people, or being what is conventionally considered to be an important, successful person. It therefore signals a realization that there is a fundamental hollowness, a basic unsatisfactoriness, in the ordinary way of living our lives. But, on the other hand, there is a realization, a faith, that the Dharma has the potential of restoring clarity, sanity, contentment, and supreme goodness to our everyday, ordinary lives. To have this disillusionment and to decide to follow the Dharma at all costs is what is meant by arousing the thought of enlightenment.

It is the determination to follow the Dharma at all costs, gladly sacrificing if necessary those things we hold most precious. Dōgen Zenji is fond of reminding us of the example of Hui-k'o, the second patriarch of Chinese Zen, who cut off his arm and offered it to Bodhidharma in order to convince him of his utmost sincerity and determination. We must therefore be prepared to risk even our health and our lives in order to acquire the Dharma, because if anything is valued more than the Dharma, we have not yet aroused the thought of enlightenment, and without this determination, we cannot acquire the Dharma. Hui-neng left his old and beloved mother in order to practice under Hung-jen, and Dōgen's own master, Ju-ching, did zazen even when his buttocks were covered with bloody sores from too much zazen. There are many stories of Zen masters who suffered from hunger and cold in order to practice Zen.

This new orientation in our lives is truly a remarkable event, then, because it is a radical reordering of priorities. But it is remarkable also because it is the appearance in our lives of a deeper and wiser mind. It is, in fact, the Buddha within us, awakening from slumber. Therefore, "arousing the thought of enlightenment" may also be said to be the "arousing of the enlightened mind," for while on the one hand it is the new determination to realize our Buddha nature, it is also the awakening of this nature itself. This is why Dōgen praises the event so extravagantly: "This thought of enlightenment, this development of practice, transcends the bounds of enlightenment and delusion. It is superior to anything else in the universe, and is preëminent in all things."[1] In the final analysis, this event is the determination of the Buddha to realize himself through us; that is, it is the appearance of the

Dharmakaya, the cosmic Buddha body, in time and space.

The prominence of the doctrine of arousing the thought of enlightenment in Dōgen's writings establishes him firmly within the Mahayana Buddhist tradition, but in the way he deepened its meaning, he arrived at what is doubtlessly the most sophisticated version of the idea in Buddhism. It is a doctrine as old as Mahayana Buddhism and is explained and extolled in almost all the major sutras and treatises of Mahayana literature. A typical treatment is to be found in Shantideva's *Bodhicaryāvatāra*.[2] In texts of this sort, the arousal of the thought of enlightenment marks the beginning of the bodhisattva's endless career of drawing closer and closer to complete, perfect enlightenment. It is an endless career because while in theory he will eventually attain this goal, in reality he will never attain it, for reasons I will mention later. The awakening of this determination to attain supreme enlightenment is accompanied by certain vows of a most serious nature, and this utter commitment starts the individual on his way through life, and all lives to come, in search of the goal. But the point to this is that the search does not really begin until the thought of enlightenment has occurred. Without the commitment, there is no practice, and without practice, there is no attainment.

Why, and how, does this thought arise in the first place? What transforms an ordinary person into an utterly committed follower of the Way? One moment we are deeply involved in pursuing success, security, and comfort, reconciled more or less to the turmoil and anguish that accompany struggle like an old mule reconciled to a treadmill. The next moment, we have abandoned those pursuits as if they were trash. Obviously there has been a serious disenchantment with these goods that are so prized by others. It is very difficult to throw them out, because the culture of which we are a part has taken great pains to indoctrinate us soundly into firmly believing that they are the most precious things to have. But this indoctrination itself is little more than a reinforcement of the innate tendency to structure our lives in such a way that we only do those things which benefit the self and avoid those things which we believe threaten or diminish it. The instinct to preserve, nourish, and enhance the self is so basic, so powerful, that it is almost impossible for most people to begin living life in any other way that is not a prolonged strategy for self-protection. Yet this is just what the bodhisattva does when he arouses the thought of enlightenment.

In Dōgen Zenji's writings, the thought of enlightenment is closely bound up with the perception of impermanence. To confront impermanence means to become radically aware of the transiency and brevity of one's own life and the other things that constitute our experience, such as friends, success, health, lovers, family, fame, pleasure, and even the great abstractions such as progress, honor, the American way of life, and so on. That is, they cease to hold a compulsive grip on us once we see that they cannot last and that we are completely incapable of hanging on to them. They constantly slip from our fingers and elude us, leaving us saddened and disappointed. We finally realize that these things are undependable and cannot satisfy us, and therefore are not fit objects of our concern. But even our own lives slip away just as quickly and relentlessly, and not only can we not take our treasures with us when we depart, we cannot even take our bodies and minds. Thus, there is a tendency to ask just how we ought to spend the few precious days allotted to us. A well-known old Buddhist verse says:

> Alas, all conditioned things are
>   impermanent;
> It is their nature to come into being and
>   then cease to be.
> For having come into being, they will
>   surely cease to be;
> Their cessation is bliss.

For Dōgen, the perception of impermanence gives rise to a determination to seek the Dharma. It is probably accurate to say that throughout the history of Buddhism, the thought of enlightenment has been connected with the perception of impermanence; in Dōgen's thinking the connection seems to have grown out of his own experience. His first confrontation with impermanence occurred when, as a boy of seven, he sat watching the smoke of the incense disappear into the air at his mother's funeral. His father had died when he was only two years old, and five years later his beloved mother had died. The smoke of the incense fading into the air must have deeply impressed him with the impermanence and brevity of those things we long for and love. "This body, hair, and skin result from the union of the sperm and egg of the father and mother. If your heart stops, will not this body be scattered on mountains and fields and turn completely into mud? Really, where can one take hold of oneself?" he asks, in the *Zuimonki*.[3] He consequently turned to the Dharma at a very young age, determined to follow it, and eventually achieved a lasting place in the succession of great Zen masters. His own attainment was the result of an intensely seeking spirit, and this seeking spirit was the result of a deep perception of impermanence. In essay after essay of the *Shōbōgenzō*, he cautions us not to waste time in the face of this inexorable impermanence, but to make haste and enter the Way.

The perception of impermanence, then, is the motivation for entering the Way and making a supreme effort. In the first essay he wrote, *Fukan zazengi*, he took pains to emphasize the fact of impermanence in a work primarily devoted to the technique of zazen:

> Do not pass over from the light to the darkness by ignoring practice and pursuing other things. Take care of this essential instrument of the Buddha Way [which is your life]. Could you ever be content with the

> sparks from a stone [when the sun is blazing
> overhead]? That is not all; your body is like a
> dew-drop on the morning grass, your life is
> as brief as a flash of lightning. Momentary
> and vain, it is lost in a moment.[4]

Here, the practice of zazen is intimately connected with the
fact of universal impermanence, for the urgency of practice is
necessitated by impermanence.

The individual turns to the Dharma because it promises
to remove the distress of life and bring about a deep recon-
ciliation with this very impermanence. The practice of the
Way is undertaken because the individual has faith in the
existence within himself of a potential for complete contentment, a contentment which is impossible to find in the pursuit of fame and profit. But it needs to be said over and over
again, so as not to misconstrue the nature of Mahayana Buddhism, that this seeking is not, in the end, simply another
form of self-gratification. It is indeed hoped, and expected,
that following the Way will lead to a better understanding of
oneself and the rest of the world, and that one will achieve a
degree of serenity and contentment. But, to go back to a question I have asked before, is any kind of progress in self-better-
ment possible as long as practice is undertaken with the
primarily selfish desire to improve one's own lot? Is the goal
of realization of one's Buddha nature compatible with a practice performed in the greedy expectation of one's own future
happiness while blithely ignoring the unhappiness of the
rest of the world? The Mahayana Buddhist answer to this
question has been "no".

The Mahayana glorification of compassion and the exal-
tation of the bodhisattva as the ideal individual are based on
this understanding, that any goodness one personally derives
from following the Dharma is a product of one's primary
aspiration to help all other beings to achieve happiness in
their lives. In other words, practice is undertaken in order to

help others, and the bodhisattva's own slow progress towards final, complete enlightenment is the result of this other-directed activity. This is the principle I mentioned in an earlier chapter: to help others is to help oneself. It may also be said that to help oneself is to help others, for real, effective help is not possible as long as we ourselves are deluded and filled with greed and hatred. Therefore, practice is done so that one is eventually capable of guiding and helping others; that is, the achievement of insight and understanding is for the purpose of helping others, not oneself. To wish to escape pain and trouble oneself and to ignore other creatures means that neither oneself nor others will find help. It is of the nature of things that we all progress together, and so we must seek the Dharma with this in mind.

Knowing, then, that a mean, selfish aspiration is not a real Buddhist aspiration, the bodhisattva begins his compassionate career with vows to emancipate all others, even before he himself is completely emancipated. The four bodhisattva vows, which are chanted daily in Zen training centers, are a public reminder of what the individual's training is all about:

> Sentient beings are innumerable; I vow to
> save them.
> Desires are inexhaustible; I vow to put an
> end to them.
> The Dharma teachings are boundless; I vow
> to master them.
> The Buddha Way is unsurpassable; I vow to
> attain it.

The person who utters these vows in all sincerity is thus the Mahayana bodhisattva. It does not matter what color the robes of the monk are, what his ordination lineage, or where he lives, for the Mahayana is a state of mind, and the bodhisattva is the person who can make these vows and really mean them. If one is able to do so, this vow itself is the arousing of the thought of enlightenment. That is what Mahayana Buddhism is all about. Dōgen Zenji makes this clear in *Hotsu bodai shin* when he says, "What is called the 'arousing of the thought of enlightenment' is the uttering of the vow to emancipate all living beings even while you yourself are not yet emancipated. When one arouses this thought, no matter how humble in appearance one is, one then becomes the guide of all beings."[5] If, as Dōgen says elsewhere, a Buddha is simply one whose main mission in the world is to guide all beings to the bliss of nirvana, then this vow must itself be the vow of the Buddha that we already are. Who else can make such a loving, selfless vow? A Buddha *is* boundless compassion.

The form of the vow indicates that the person who makes it will refuse the ultimate prize of complete enlightenment until and unless all other beings attain it first. And this vow is not restricted only to human, or even sentient beings, but finally includes trees, grass, shrubs, that is to say, every thing that lives. This is because Mahayana compassion and the bodhisattva's vow are not directed solely toward the human realm, for if it excluded nonhuman beings, it would not be perfect compassion, nor would the vow be unconditional. It is not that Mahayana Buddhism is inhuman or nonhuman (let alone antihuman); rather, it is transhuman, for the cycle of birth and death and its suffering includes all living things, not just the human part of life. Now obviously the number of beings to be saved is indeed vast, even innumerable, as the vow says, and because the bodhisattva is really only a human being, and limited in the way all conditioned beings are, it would seem that in reality there will never be a time when his work is finished. Thus, in making the vow, he destines himself to be forever excluded from the ultimate goal. In life after life, in all the realms of suffering, the bodhisattva works ceaselessly to save all others, whole he himself is never completely free of pain and delusion. One of the startling paradoxes of Mahayana Buddhism is that it is the bodhisattva alone, skillful, wise, and compassionate, who will never attain full, perfect Buddhahood, for while others go on, he remains behind.

But what, after all, is a Buddha? What, after all, is perfect enlightenment? In the answer to this lies another paradox which points to the character of Mahayana Buddhism. Buddhists over two thousand years ago asked these same questions, and in answering them created the movement within Buddhism which we now know as Mahayana. True enlightenment, they said, is not the complete, final cutting off of the round of rebirth and suffering and the entering of final nirvana (*nirupadhiśesa nirvāna*). Instead, one achieves the only real enlightenment precisely at that point when, out of compassion for the suffering of living beings, one deliberately refuses to attain the stage of final nirvana and enlightenment unless all other living beings attain it too. Thus, the paradox is that in refusing what is traditionally considered to be the ultimate goal of Buddhism and choosing to remain behind to serve as a guide, one really acquires the only true enlightenment and nirvana.[6]

It cannot really be otherwise, for if enlightenment is, among other things, complete selflessness, then only when we have rid ourselves of selfishness to the point where we are no longer selfishly greedy even for the fruits of training do we really reach the exalted goal of Buddhism. In gladly giving it up, we acquire it. The arousing of the thought of enlightenment, then, which Dōgen says is nothing other than this compassionate vow, is really a remarkable, wonderful occasion. It is remarkable and wonderful because the very ability to make such a vow and mean it most sincerely must be the appearance in one's life of a selflessness and compassion which are truly Buddha-like. It is, according to Dōgen Zenji, the manifestation of our Buddha nature.

In Buddhism, the ultimate is *bodhi*, which is also Buddhahood. If the highest, perfect enlightenment [*anuttara samyak sambodhi*] is compared with the initial arousing of the thought of enlightenment, it is like comparing the great conflagration at the time of the world's end with the light of a firefly. Still, if one arouses the thought of enlightenment, the thought of emancipating all other living beings even before one is emancipated oneself, there is no difference between the two. A Buddha is simply a person who thinks, 'How can I cause beings to enter the supreme Dharma and rapidly become Buddhas?' This is the life of a Tathagata.[7]

But even this exertion of one's own inherent enlightenment nature in the perpetual act of helping all others to realize their enlightenment nature is not the final truth. After all, Śākyamuni did not dedicate his life simply to helping us to become completely enlightened and to escape the world of karma and rebirth. He taught us, rather, to teach others to teach others, until such time as the world is full of beings whose sole aim in life is to be of service to others. Thus, to arouse the thought of enlightenment is not just to make a determination to enlighten all beings; it is the determination to motivate all living beings to motivate all living beings, and on and on. "Benefiting living beings," says Dōgen, "means causing living beings to arouse the thought of emancipating all others even before each is himself emancipated. We cannot become Buddhas in any other way than through the power of causing this thought (of emancipating all others before oneself is emancipated) to arise in others."[8] Thus, Dōgen in effect universalizes the bodhisattva vow and the thought of enlightenment, and his vision is that of a world in which all beings are primarily motivated by this vow. It cannot be otherwise according to him, for if any being enters the Dharma for himself, and not for others, it is not the Dharma and he has not entered. To practice the Dharma is to "drop off mind and body," and when mind and body have been forgotten to the extent that we are no longer selfishly motivated to acquire even the wonderful prize of enlightenment for ourselves, we have really entered the Dharma. We have aroused the thought of enlightenment.

This arousing of the thought of enlightenment is then expressed in countless ways, all of which are "wonderful practice" based on this deeper consciousness. Consequently, the thought of enlightenment opens us up to, and frees us to, many activities which were impossible before. Because events are known by the enlightened mind itself, we no longer approach experience in the greedy or fearful manner characteristic of ordinary life. For the most part, this enlightened activity takes the form of gratitude to the Buddha and a desire to give to others whatever is within one's power to give.

It is the enlightened mind which arouses the thought of enlightenment. The meaning of this phrase, 'it is the enlightened mind which arouses the thought of enlightenment,' is that one makes a *stūpa* with a blade of grass; one makes a sutra scroll with a rootless tree; one honors the Buddha with a grain of sand; one honors the Buddha with a bowl of water in which rice has been soaked. One gives a handful of food to a living being, or offers five flowers to the Tathagata. These are all forms of arousing the thought of enlightenment. Arousing the thought of enlightenment means following the encouragement of others, doing good even to the slight extent you are capable of, and bowing to the Buddha even while you are being annoyed by demons. And it is not only these.

Arousing the thought of enlightenment also means knowing that your home is not your true home, leaving the home life, entering the mountains and practicing the Buddha Way, and practicing with faith in a teacher or by reading the scriptures. It means making an image of the Buddha, building a *stūpa*, reading the scriptures, being mindful of the Buddha, preaching the Dharma to living beings, visiting a teacher and asking questions, and sitting cross-legged doing zazen. It is also bowing to the Buddha, Dharma, and Sangha and repeating 'Homage to the Buddha'.[9]

Why are all these activities the same as arousing the thought of enlightenment? As Dōgen defines it, arousing the thought of enlightenment is truly a momentous affair. Yet, here it is said to be the same as doing zazen, offering someone a morsel of food, offering a few flowers to the Buddha, and so on.

Why this is so will be clearer if we remember how hard it is for us to do these things. It is hard for ordinary people to give rather than take. It is hard to perform what seem to be meaningless or unprofitable acts, such as bowing to the Buddha or offering him incense. Zazen itself is hard because we do not really believe we can gain anything from it; it is lost time and not much fun. It is really a difficult thing to do, to offer a few flowers and bow to the Buddha. Obviously, the person who can easily do these things looks at life in a different way than most people do, for he can now do things without weighing them in terms of profit and loss. He has aroused the thought of enlightenment, which means he gives what he is capable of giving, however small and inexpensive, and he honors the Buddha and shows his gratitude in many ways. It is therefore true that to honor the Buddha with whatever poor thing one has and to give freely to others without

45

any thought of benefit or loss is a sure sign that one has aroused the thought of enlightenment.

Because this is what it means to arouse the thought of enlightenment, the act is performed in many ways, some of which I have discussed in other chapters. It is, for instance, faith, because both faith and arousing the thought of enlightenment are nothing more than an unshakable trust in the truth and value of the Buddha's teaching and a determination to live one's life in conformity with that teaching. It is also identical with home departure, for real home departure (as I will show in a later chapter) is a complete renunciation of fame, fortune, power, and security, and a new orientation towards the Buddha and his teaching. In other words, arousing the thought of enlightenment, faith, and home departure are all forms of what Dōgen Zenji called "dropping off mind and body."

We can go through all the proper motions, doing Zen in a formalistic way, but it is not good enough. It is clear that Dōgen had an extremely rigorous definition of what it means to follow the Dharma. It is no easy thing to really follow the Way. We can shave our heads, burn mountains of incense, give up sex, meat, and alcohol, and sit on a meditation pillow until it crumbles to dust, but if we have not aroused the thought of enlightenment, we are still mountains and rivers away from Dharma. It is what is in the heart that finally counts. If, in the perception of impermanence and suffering, one turns one's back on ordinary values, turns to the Buddha and his teachings as the real refuge of oneself and others, and places foremost in one's life the task of guiding all beings to enlightenment even before oneself is enlightened, one has aroused the thought of enlightenment and truly started out on the endless Path for the first time. The Buddha within has awakened, stretched, arisen, and gone forth to do his life's work.

# NOTES

1. *Hotsu bodai shin*, quoted by Okada Gihō, in *Shōbōgenzō shisō taikei* (Tokyo: Hosei University Press, 1965), Vol. 6, p. 116.

2. *Entering the Path of Enlightenment: The Bodhicāryāvatāra of the Buddhist Poet Śantideva*, trans. Marion L. Matics (New York: MacMillan Co., 1970).

3. *A Primer of Sōtō Zen (Shōbōgenzō Zuimonki)*, trans. Masunaga Reihō (Honolulu: East-West Center Press, 1971), p. 62.

4. *Fukan zazengi*, quoted in *Dōgen shū (Nihon no shisō*, Vol. 2), ed. Tamaki Koshirō (Tokyo: Chikuma Shobo, 1969), p. 55.

5. *Hotsu bodai shin*, in *Shōbōgenzō shisō taiei*, Vol. 6, p. 113.

6. *The Lankāvatāra Sūtra*, trans. Daisetz T. Suzuki (London: Routledge and Kegan Paul, 1932), p. 184. "Mahāmati, when the Bodhisattvas face and perceive the happiness of the samadhi of perfect tranquillization, they are moved with the feeling of love and sympathy owing to their original vows, and they become aware of the part they are to perform as regard the [ten] inexhaustible vows. Thus, they do not enter Nirvana. But the fact is that they are already in Nirvana, because in them there is no arising of discrimination."

7. *Hotsu bodai shin*, in *Shōbōgenzō shisō taikei*, Vol. 6, p. 118.

8. *Ibid.*, p. 119.

9. *Hotsu mujō shin*, in *Zenyaku shōbōgenzō*, trans. Nakamura Sōichi (Tokyo: Seishin Shobo, 1972–73), Vol. 3, p. 173.

# FOUR

*The Problem of Karma*

Every person is faced with the problem of karma. We can escape neither karma nor its consequences *(karma-phala)*, for there is no place we can go where karma (literally, "act", "deed", "a doing") does not occur or where we are immune from its consequences. One of the oldest Buddhist texts, the *Dhammapāda*, says that pain follows karma as the plow follows the footprints of the ox. It is a very old teaching in Buddhism, and it is accurate to say that Buddhism as a system of ideas and practices has throughout its twenty-five centuries of existence been concerned mainly with the problem of karma. It is important also to understand that Zen Buddhism is not Buddhist psychotherapy, a method of self-realization, a tranquilizer, nor the key to a life of irresponsible "freedom", but is the Buddhist means of dealing with karma and its consequences.

Karma is defined in Buddhism as volitional action, meaning any act, good or bad, which is preceded by will or intention. Therefore, the act may be a physical one, such as giving a gift, or a vocal one, such as lying, and if the act is preceded by an intention to give a gift or to lie, then karma has occurred. Such acts are almost always motivated by either desire or hatred, which are the content of the intention, so that the giving, injury, deceit, and so forth are expressions of hatred or desire (even if it be a desire to do good). Buddhism teaches that an act of this nature leaves an impression or residue in the mind and that at some later time, this residue will bring about some result or consequence in the life of the doer or in the lives of others. The psychological insight of Buddhism is that we are unable to perform acts of this nature without their leaving some influence in our lives. Volitional acts are a form of energy which radiates outward from the doer and affects both himself and others. The murderer may never be apprehended and punished by civil authorities, but the deed survives in the present, and sometime, somewhere, the energy of the past act will have an effect on both the murderer and others. The energy is never lost.

Karma is therefore a problem for all of us because it is human to act out of desire and loathing. Actually, however, the problem may be extended to include also those factors in our lives for which we are not personally responsible, that is, the many conditions we are each subject to by virtue of existing in a world of other entities. These conditions are countless and all affect our lives to one degree or another. They include the climate, the economic system of our society and the larger world, the quality of our minds, the bodies we have inherited from our parents, the food we eat, education, gravity, people, and so on. In fact, every entity in the universe in one way or another conditions our own personal existence in some way. And because we are conditioned in this way, we are subject to many limitations; we can never exceed the intellectual capacity of our brains, for instance, nor, as living things, can we be completely free from sickness, pain, old age, the loss of physical and mental powers, nor, of course, the ultimate terror, death and nothingness. These things are our common lot as conditioned beings; they come to us despite our loathing of them, and like the karma mentioned earlier, they follow us wherever we go. There is thus no real avoidance of these things, which are part and parcel of our existence. Thus, the human (and nonhuman) problem goes beyond volitional acts and their consequences. The more general problem is that of dealing effectively with those things which come to us whether we like them or not. "Flowers fall, giving rise to longing," says Dōgen, "and weeds flourish, arousing our loathing."

The problem is not an imagined one, nor the product of a mind which is incapable of facing life's inevitabilities. It may be said that all people are aware of the problem to one degree or another. Banding together in tribes or other communities, for example, is not so much a reflection of mutual love as it is the recognition that many hands and minds together can accomplish what the lone individual cannot in fighting off cave bears, hunger, natural calamities, and the like. Religion also may be seen as one response to the fact of our limitations. It is probably true that most people live lives of fear and insecurity and that most acts they perform are really reactions to threats against their security. It is therefore not a question of whether people are aware of the great problem of life and death but rather a question of the effectiveness of the means they employ to deal with it, for each of us tries to deal with it in one way or another.

However, it is a losing battle and we know it. Much pathological behavior is probably due to a realization that we cannot really ward off these invaders, for the weapons we employ are ineffective. All weapons are ineffective, finally. Then what can we do?

*Shunjū* ("Spring and Fall"), which is one of the essays from *Shōbōgenzō* translated in this volume, addresses this problem, the problem of cause and effect. A monk approaches the Zen master Tung-shan (Tōzan) and asks, "When the heat of summer and the cold of winter arrive, how can we escape them?" His question is, of course, How can we escape old age, sickness, death, and the like? Tung-shan replies, "Why don't you go some place where there is no heat or cold?" "Where is this place where there is no heat or cold?" asks the monk. Tung-shan answers, "When it is hot, the heat kills the monk; when it is cold, the cold kills the monk." Now, the monk accepts the fact that the heat and cold will come. There is no chance that they will not. We will be hot in summer and cold in winter, whether we like it or not. Yet Tung-shan says that there is a place where there is neither heat nor cold. The question every Zen student asks when he practices zazen is, Where is this place where there is no heat or cold?

The answer to this question takes many forms, as I remarked above when I said that everyone responds to the problem of life and death in some way. One Zen master said, "When it is hot, fan yourself, and when it is cold, get closer to the heater." This seems to be a practical way of solving the problem, but Dōgen says that it is the answer of a child. It is an ineffective and immature answer, as children's answers usually are, for in reality there are no fans or heaters. All the chemicals and machinery of medical science will not ward off eventual deterioration and death, and the alcohol and other drugs we take to eliminate stress only create new suffering. Karmic consequences are inevitable. Children's solutions to problems are not only ineffective but often compound the problem, yet most people attack the problem of life and death as if they were still children.

Tung-shan says that there is a "place", however, where there is no heat or cold. It has no geographical location, of course, unless it is "nowhere", which is everywhere. It is a "place" where even though it is mid-summer and we perspire freely, we are truly free from the heat, for when we are free from the heat even as we are drenched with perspiration, we have found Tung-shan's "place". The bodhisattva who is willing, even eager, to be reborn forever in the realms of suffering—the human world, the world of animals, the purgatories—has found this "place" right in the very midst of turmoil, anxiety, frustration, competition, terror, death, and all the rest. This is why Buddhism is truly a human religion, because it does not attempt to distract man from the reality of sentient existence by promising a future nirvāna or heaven which is exempt from the conditions of sentient life. It rather demands that we see our lives with clear vision and find freedom and perfect goodness within and through the conditions which make up the fabric of our lives. Consequently, there is no promise of Utopia, or a restored Eden, no promise of escape from conditionality in some transcendental world. Buddhism therefore demands that we abandon all self-deception, all myths and daydreams, all beguiling fairy stories which prevent us from truly understanding the nature of our lives. There is, finally, only "this", as the Zen master Ta-mei told his students as he lay dying and heard a squirrel chatter on the roof. The blossoms fall despite our longing; the weeds flourish despite our loathing, so what can we do about it?

*Shinjin inga* ("Deep Faith in Cause and Effect"), also translated in this volume, is deeply concerned with this question. The essay begins with one of the best-known and important koans, "Pai-chang and the Fox." Every day when the Zen master Pai-chang spoke to the monks in the lecture hall, an old man would listen with them and then depart when they departed. One day when the monks went out, however, the old man remained behind. "Who are you?" asked Pai-chang. "I am not human," answered the old man, "I am a fox spirit. Long ago, I was the abbot of a monastery on this spot. One day, a monk asked me, 'Is an enlightened person subject to the law of cause and effect?' and I answered, 'He is not.' As a result of that, I have been reborn as a fox for five hundred lifetimes. Please say something now which will free me from the body of the fox. Is the enlightened individual subject to the law of cause and effect?" Pai-chang answered, "He is not exempt from the law of cause and effect." Thereupon, the old man told Pai-chang that he was now freed from the body of the fox and requested that the fox's body be buried with the honors due a monk. Pai-chang said he would, and later he and the other monks found the fox's body and disposed of it in the proper manner.

Dōgen Zenji speaks approvingly of Pai-chang's answer, for the whole essay is a sustained assertion of the reality and inflexibility of the law of cause and effect. No one is exempt, even abbots and Zen masters, as the five hundred lives as a fox clearly demonstrates. And Dōgen makes the interesting point later in the essay that even after being freed from the body of the fox, the old man would have to be reborn someplace else, because there is no relaxation of the law of cause and effect. Dōgen's approval of Pai-chang's answer seems to reaffirm the fact of conditionedness for all entities, living and otherwise. Even the enlightened individual perspires in summer and shivers in winter. His toothache hurts terribly, he grows old and possibly helpless, and in the end, like everyone else, he ends up as nothing but a puff of gray smoke over the crematorium. Perhaps he even becomes a fox. Buddhism cannot promise us otherwise.

Then why practice and follow the Dharma? If both the enlightened person and the deluded fool end up as ashes and become foxes, why devote one's entire life to self-denial, hard discipline, and the pursuit of something called "enlightenment"? The reason is that Zen does promise that there is a "place" where we can be free from the toothache, the loss, the old age and death, even as we deeply experience the pain, the aging process, and the dying. Tung-shan says, "When it is hot, the heat kills the monk; when it is cold, the cold kills the monk." This statement is sometimes translated from the Japanese as, "When it is hot, be completely hot; when it is cold, be completely cold," which is precisely what Tung-shan means. In other words, instead of vainly seeking to escape the conditions which constitute our lives by means of flight—spiritual or otherwise—one finds a real and meaningful freedom from this conditionedness through a radical, profound affirmation of one's very conditionedness. Thus, as Dōgen tells us in various places, when you are alive, be completely alive, and when you are dying, die thoroughly, with nothing else intruding into the living or dying. This is in fact the lesson one learns in the *jijiyū zammai* which Dōgen praises so strongly. By means of an absolute oneness with the circumstances themselves, no matter what they are, one paradoxically becomes free from them. Dōgen calls this *gūjin*, a difficult term to translate, but which means something like "total realization," "total understanding," "total manifestation," or "total exertion." Looked at from the angle of the person who experiences the situation, it means that one identifies one hundred percent with the circumstance. Looked at from the standpoint of the situation itself, the situation is totally manifested or exerted without obstruction or contamination.

There is another old Zen story which illustrates this total at-one-ment with circumstances. A young monk was disillusioned with Zen when he heard his revered master scream in pain and fear as he was being murdered by thieves. The young man contemplated leaving Zen training, feeling that if his old master screamed in the face of death, Zen itself must be a fraud. However, before he was able to leave, another teacher taught him something of what Zen is all about and removed his misconceptions. "Fool!" exclaimed the teacher, "the object of Zen is not to kill all feelings and become anesthetized to pain and fear. The object of Zen is to free us to scream loudly and fully when it is time to scream." This is, I believe, what Dōgen Zenji means by *gūjin*, the total exertion of any circumstance. When one thing is totally manifested or totally exerted, nothing else exists but that thing, for all of reality is focused into that single circumstance. "When one side is illuminated," says Dōgen, "the other side is darkened." That is to say, when one becomes hot or cold, pained or grief stricken, completely, with nothing added, then being *nothing but* pain, heat, cold, grief, or joy (the "other side is darkened"), one has found Tung-shan's "place" where there is neither heat nor cold. What is not added to the circumstance is of course the self. How else can we be free from conditions? There are in reality no dentists, pain killers, or anything else when it comes to the inevitabilities of our existence, because we exist, and to exist means to be subject to conditions (and to act as a condition for others).

For this reason, Dōgen Zenji's Zen is a most interesting, profound approach to the problem of life and death. It may be questioned whether it is a religion at all, at least insofar as "religion" is commonly understood. Even less likely is it an Oriental form of mysticism, for none of the well-known mystics, either Eastern or Western, has ever spoken of his or her experience in these terms. Dōgen's Zen is as far removed from the ecstasies of Theresa of Avila or John of the Cross as any experience can be. Nor does it parallel in any significant way the experiences of Eckhart or even some of the more contemporary Hindu figures such as Aurobindo or Ramakrishna. The experience of mysticism is almost always described in terms of transcendence of some kind and is frequently coupled with ecstasy. But there is no sign of transcendence in Dōgen's Zen, unless it is self-transcendence. Rather, it immerses the individual even more deeply into the flow of worldly existence, affirming and transforming worldly experience itself, and completely rejecting the dualisms that are either implicit or explicit in the utterances of the mystics. There is no distinction between things which are holy and nonholy, worldly and unworldly, sacred and profane, and consequently there are no transcendental realms into which one merges, leaving a presumably fallen and impure world behind. There is something singularly nonholy, completely ordinary, in Dōgen's Zen. We must recall the words of Bodhidharma again when he was asked by the Emperor Wu what the holy teaching of Buddhism is. "Vast emptiness, and nothing holy about it," replied Bodhidharma. Indeed, there is nothing holy about it, at least as we understand holiness. What, after all, do the patriarchal masters do? "Eat rice and drink tea," says Dōgen in *Kajō*.

However, there is eating rice and there is eating rice, and the ordinary daily experience of the Zen masters, while apparently no different from our own, is in fact transformed by a special insight. For what Zen teaches us is not the renunciation or rejection of worldly experience—the "profane"—but its transformation. It is a radically realistic solution to the problem of samsara, for instead of trying to go beyond the world, the individual learns to resee and renew worldly experience itself. In traditional Buddhist terminology, this renewal and reseeing is none other than the realization that all being is the Buddha. It is not that some certain aspects of life are the Buddha while others are not, resulting in a world which is really divided up between the sacred and profane. That would be a very unbuddhistic dualism. The Buddha is present in everything. He is present in loss and failure, betrayal, the falling of flower petals, brain tumors, the hanged criminal, the collapse of dynasties, and in the extinguishing of suns. All these things are the inevitable result of the law of cause and effect, and that law begets terrors as well as beauties. There is no other reality, no matter how much we may long for one and dream of it; like it or not, we are stuck with this one reality. Therefore, there is no place to which to escape, nor would there be any need to escape if such a place did exist, for we can, with determination and effort, see and understand this reality in such a way that we can affirm it just as it is.

Where is this "place"? It is not "here", if "here" is some special place or thing distinct from some other place or thing. Nor is "here" this world as it is experienced by ordinary people, a "here" which is full of turmoil, struggle, pain, death. Nor is it "there", if "there" is some distant, ideal world beyond the clouds, where there is eternal peace and tranquillity and where disease, loss, change, frustration, and the rest are completely absent. *Where* is the place, which is neither here nor there; that is, the place is "where". "Where" is indeed anyplace the self and its discriminations and distinctions are not, which is to say it is this very world transformed by the penetrating light of *prajñā* insight. It is this world as true emptiness, this world as Buddha. This is what the Buddha meant in the *Lotus Sutra* when he said that when ordinary people see the world consumed by raging fires at the end of the cosmic eon, he sees it as remaining cool and delightful, inhabited by humans and celestial beings. It is therefore a matter of how we see it, a certain perspective.

Buddhism has always been the way of understanding, as well as the way of compassion, which is, after all, simply the active expression of understanding. It is also the way of awakening, the implication being that we are all asleep, stupefied. We do not know what life is, what death is, or what we are. We are totally confused about time and have childish notions about the eternal. We are in utter darkness when we reflect on our relationship with everything else, and we are pathological in our assignment of values and judgements to events. It is therefore imperative that we make the supreme effort of questioning everything we think we really know. If we can see and understand, then we have found the key to fully living the only life we will ever have. Also, we will have finally grown up when we abandon our naive, childish fantasies about utopias, transcendental realms, eternal peace and comfort in distant heavens, or any other dream which prevents us from facing reality. To do this, we must understand what our life is, as well as that larger life of which ours is only a part. What is it, then? A chant used in Zen ceremony says,

> The whole universe is an ocean of dazzling
> light,
> And on it dance the waves of life and
> death.

What does it mean when it says that the whole universe is an ocean of dazzling light? Why is it so difficult to see that light? How can we learn to see it?

The object then is not transcendence but transformation, but this does not mean that there is no need for self-transcendence. The self must be bypassed or transcended, for it is the insistent intrusion of the self and its needs which makes our life boring or terrible. However, it is not transcendence if by that we mean removing ourselves from this reality, getting out of the stream of cause and effect and the process of action and consequence. Much Buddhism prior to Dōgen Zenji did in fact see the Dharma as having this function, particularly in Indian Buddhism. Western religions traditionally have conceived of a world beyond the world, a world which is diametrically opposite the lower world in having no death, pain, separation, disease, impurity, sin, and so forth. It is a changeless world, static and monotonous in its eternal bliss and ease. The upturned, longing gaze of a Catherine of Sienna in Western religious art expresses this belief most concretely. But then notice the portraits of Zen masters doing zazen with eyes closed or eyes open but still looking within. They express perfectly the ancient Buddhist teaching that the world of samsara is itself nirvana. They see it as nirvana because they see it from the vantage point of that "place" or "ground" (both merely being metaphors) which lies beneath and preceeds self, attachments, and discrimination. In that place they have found freedom from life and death (samsara) while remaining deeply immersed in it.

With this kind of freedom, the problems of samsara, karmic consequences, conditionality, and limitation cease to be problems, though we are not removed from them. Enlightenment will not literally free us from rebirth, and like the old man who spoke to Pai-chang, we still may end up later as foxes, maggots, cockroaches, hungry ghosts, and the like. The old man was reborn after being freed from the body of the fox, and what fate may have lain in store for him, attached as he was to human form and disliking his foxness? Zen cannot

guarantee that we will escape these possibilities (or proba-
bilities), but it can guarantee that with diligent effort we can
come to see that there is nothing wrong with being a fox. May
not the five hundred years which the old abbot spent as a fox
have been delightful? Does a fox regret his foxness and long
to be a human, or is a fox just as perfect in his foxness as a
human being is in his humanness? Mumon says, in his commentary on "Pai-chang and the Fox" in *Mumonkan* (Case 2):

> "Not falling into causation." Why was he
> turned into a fox? "Not ignoring causation."
> Why was he released from the fox body? If
> you have an eye to see through this, then
> you will know that the former head of the
> monastery did enjoy his five hundred happy
> blessed lives as a fox.[1]

Looked at from a purely human perspective, it is better to be
human than a fox, but looked at in the light of truth, both are
equally perfect. Each thing equally manifests its Buddha nature.

Pai-chang was certainly correct in saying that the enlightened individual is subject to the law of cause and effect,
and the old abbot's five hundred years as a fox bears eloquent
testimony to this fact. But was rebirth as a fox a punishment or
retribution for speaking inaccurately? If the law is the law, the
old abbot had to be reborn as something, and why not a fox?
And was the previous abbot's comment really inaccurate? It is
untrue if it means that the enlightened person cannot become
a fox, but it is not untrue if it means that the fox can enjoy his
foxness and be free from it. Zen abbots die like everyone else,
and even Śākyamuni grew old, suffered from dysentery, and
died from it, but in a sense, they are no longer subject to the
law of cause and effect. The enlightened individual is free
from life and death through the very act of totally affirming
and confirming life and death, which brings us back again to
Tung-shan's "place" where there is no heat or cold.

Understanding also means self-understanding, and in a real sense, Zen training is a process of self-understanding. It shows us what we really are, apart from our illusions. Every person who truly undertakes Zen training does so in the belief that there is something wrong with him or her, because the reality of their lives does not measure up to some idealized, perfect self-image which can be attained through spiritual training. Zen training shows us first of all what we really are, our real personality as distinct from the projected idealization. Then, with luck and hard work, we discover that what we really are is good enough and has been all along. However, the training is necessary if we are to really know this. In this sense, Zen training is also a process of self-acceptance. I do not mean by this a simple (and self-serving) acceptance of one's attachments, hatreds, jealousies, laziness, deceit, and so on, a situation which one accepts with resignation and some sense of relief because now nothing has to be done about it. This is mere self-indulgence and irresponsibility. One may eventually discover that he or she is perfectly all right and always has been, but the training and realization that lead to that discovery are absolutely necessary. It is necessary to discover the real nature of attachment, hatred, laziness, and so on. Self-acceptance is also a matter of learning that one is a conditioned being whose nature it is to be born, to experience, to be subject to conditions beyond one's control, to feel, to suffer, and to die. It is also the acceptance of oneself as an entity whose nature it is to be a condition for the existence of countless other entities also, with all that this implies with regard to personal conduct. It is the acceptance of oneself as really a rather ordinary, nonprivileged being living in the only world there is, and of the fact that comfortable dreams and fantasies are only ways of avoiding facing it. To learn this is to understand what one is and what one's fellow creatures are, and to understand in this way is to find that "place" where there is neither heat nor cold.

# NOTES

1. Shibayama Zenkei, *Zen Comments on the Mumonkan* (New York: Harper and Row, 1976), p. 33.

# FIVE

## *The Scriptures*

*Nyorai zenshin*, which is translated as "The Tathagata's Whole Body," is concerned with scriptural literature, with *stūpas*, which are the funerary mounds which enclose the ashes of important Buddhist figures, and with the whole body of the Buddha. It is also about practice, as are all the chapters of *Shōbōgenzō* translated in this volume. It does not concern practice in the sense that it prescribes proper posture and the like, but many things have a bearing on practice besides formal zazen activities, as the many chapters of *Shōbōgenzō* indicate. *Shōji* ("Life and Death"), for instance, is really more of a philosophical discussion of life and death; *Kannon* ("Avalokiteśvara") is concerned with the nature of enlightened activity. There are many essays like these in *Shōbōgenzō*, and while they are not directly concerned with practice in the way, for instance, that *Gyōji* or *Fukan zazengi* are, they nevertheless are aids to practice. They help us to avoid misconceptions about the nature of practice and enlightenment, the nature of existence, the nature of the Buddha, and so on, and in so doing, they serve to clarify the true nature of our lives and practice. In the same way, *Nyorai zenshin*, in talking about stupas, sutras, and the essence of the Buddha, presents us with several important ideas which help orient us in our practice.

First, the point is made very strongly in *Nyorai zenshin* that the true remains of the Buddha's body are found in the sutras. It has been the custom in Buddhist countries ever since the time of Śākyamuni to cremate the dead, and the Buddha himself was cremated in this manner. Usually, all that remains of the body are a few small fragments of bone and some ashes, called *sharīra* and often referred to as "relics." They are considered to be the essence of the dead body, though not a metaphysical essence or self. These relics were frequently enshrined in a stupa (or *pagoda,* as they were called in China) and presumably Śākyamuni's relics were enshrined in the same way. But the point which Dōgen Zenji makes in *Nyorai zenshin* is that the true relics do not consist of the ashes and bone entombed in the stupa, but rather the true remains of Śākyamuni consist of the teachings which are enshrined in the scriptures. In other words, the real body of Śākyamuni consists of his Dharma, and the only place we can find it is in the scriptures.

Now it is true, of course, that Zen speaks of a "direct transmission from mind to mind," in which Śākyamuni's enlightenment is duplicated wordlessly in each generation of individuals, primarily by means of the interaction of master and disciple. But this direct transmission refers to the enlightenment itself; Buddhism—the system of practices and ideas which make up the context of, and vehicle for, the enlightenment experience—is itself transmitted only, or primarily, in the sutras and in the commentaries which help us read the sutras. If the sutras ceased to exist, or if the individual remained ignorant of them, then there would be no Buddhism, no Dharma. If Zen is Zen Buddhism, then the only place we can encounter Śākyamuni's life teaching, which we call "Buddhism," is in the sutras. They enshrine the whole body of the Tathagata.

One of the things which characterizes Dōgen's Zen is his attempt to restore the importance of the sutras by countering the tendency that arose in Chinese Zen to severely devaluate the status of the scriptures. Bodhidharma's "no dependence on words or letters" is either the source of this high-handed disregard of the scriptures or maybe a later literary expression of it, but in any case, "no dependence on words or letters" has come to serve as an ideological basis for disparaging reading and learning, glorifying ignorance and mental laziness, and ignoring the scriptures. But Bodhidharma's verse speaks only of "dependence" on literature, not of reading and using it. That is, it does not council us to disregard and disrespect it, but merely warns of dependence. Early Chinese Zen was conscious of itself as constituting a radical departure from traditional Chinese Buddhism, which was oriented almost exclusively toward scriptural study, lecturing, exegesis, writing learned commentaries, and so on. Pre-Zen and, later, non-Zen Buddhism therefore tended to be academic and scholarly, with practically no emphasis on practice, so that the monasteries greatly resembled Western universities. Zen was a departure because it originated in the knowledge that practice and attainment, not theoretical knowledge and scholarship, are the real heart of Buddhism. Bodhidharma's famous verse is an advertisement of the nature of this new Chinese Buddhism, and it simply says that the emphasis is on practice and attainment, and not on scholarship. However, as time passed, a number of mad hatters in Zen monasteries either forgot, or chose to ignore, the fact that it was not a strict matter of either/or, but rather one of emphasis, and in their extreme interpretation of the verse claimed that reading the scriptures is harmful, spoke disparagingly of them, and in general behaved as if the Buddha's words were like poison serpents. The familiar painting of Hui-neng gleefully tearing up a copy of the *Diamond Sutra* graphically portrays the excesses to which this attitude was taken.

This was only a tendency on the part of one segment of the Zen community at one historical period, but it gave birth to a literature (ironically) which has perpetuated the notion among many who are disposed to believe it anyway that anyone involved in Zen practice should have nothing to do with books in general and Buddhist scriptural literature in particular. The point has been made by one Zen master that Bodhidharma's statement only means that one should not be *used by* the scriptures, not that one should not *use* them. If one does nothing but read the scriptures, this is not real Zen practice, but there are many ways in which a careful study of the scriptures can enhance and strengthen the central practice. For centuries, Zen monastic compounds contained a library as one of the buildings, and Japanese Zen continued this practice. The library was the place where Zen Buddhists could learn something about the Buddhism they professed.

Dōgen attempts to restore the importance of the scriptures when he says that the sutra is the whole body of the Buddha. But this, while instructive, is only part of the story. For the question is, Where can the whole body of the Buddha *not* be found? In *Nyorai zenshin*, when the Buddha instructs the bodhisattva Bhaisajyarāja to venerate the stupa, he says that the relics of the Buddha need not be placed in it, because it already contains the whole body of the Buddha. Of course the whole body of the Buddha is already in the stupa because the whole body is everywhere.

Scholars have pointed out that the simple mound of earth which once covered the remains of important figures gradually evolved into a much more complex structure, with a brick or stone facing covering the earth mound, a walkway which surrounded it on which pilgrims could circumambulate, and a square fence around the whole structure, with an entryway penetrating the fence on each of the four sides. Looked at from above, the stupa can be seen to resemble the structure of a *mandala,* and this was no mere accident, for just as the center of the mandala symbolizes the Buddha essence which occupies both the center of cosmic reality and the psychophysical center of the human being, so did the stupa come to portray this same understanding of reality. In this way, both the mandala and the stupa, in their similar structures, symbolize the structure of both the cosmos and the psyche of the living being, and the center of the mandala and the relics buried beneath ground level in the very center of the stupa represent the Dharma body of the Buddha. The image is that if a universally-pervading reality which exists in embryo form within each entity. The whole body of the Tathāgata is enshrined in each entity, and therefore the relics do not need to be placed in the stupa. Thus, since, in a manner of speaking, the whole universe is the stupa, and each one of us is the stupa, there is nothing which should not be venerated.

This is important for the individual to keep in mind as he undertakes Zen practice, because otherwise, we can easily fall into the error of assuming that there are only certain special places and events in which the whole body of the Buddha can be found. And we need to remember further that Zen practice itself has as its goal the overcoming of a false dualism whereby we tend to discriminate between things which are worthy and unworthy, sacred and profane, good and bad, Buddha and non-Buddha, and so on. We then forget that the whole universe is the stupa which contains the whole body of the Buddha, and that as a consequence, the Buddha is found in other people—even the ones we do not like very much— in crowded, noisy cities (and not just in the country with frogs and crickets), in the kitchen in the sink full of dirty dishes, in the fussing child, and, to be sure, in the scriptures and other literature. In forgetting this and getting ourselves even more deeply entwined with dualisms and discrimination, we do not really practice Zen in the most effective manner. All these things, and many more, testify in their own way to the presence of the Buddha, but learning this is perhaps the hardest thing of all to do. In his *Buddhist Sermons on Christian Texts*, R. H. Blyth says, with regard to the Christian Biblical passage, "They rest not day and night, saying Holy, Holy, Holy, Lord God Almighty" (*Revelation* IV,8):

> This is the silence of a myriad whirling suns, the shriek of a knife on a plate, a tale told by an idiot, the yelling of a wounded soldier on the battlefield begging to be put out of his misery. The lapping of waves on the rocks of some far-off island, the farting of the bean eater, the air-raid siren,—all these praise the Lord God Almighty with no uncertain voice. But almost all men are as deaf to the meaning of these voices as they are to that of a Bach fugue.[1]

We kill the Buddha when we reserve only nice, special places for his presence.

It is not that just a fragment of the Buddha is to be found in the kitchen, or in the scriptures, or in the screams of the man dying in pain; each is the whole body of the Buddha just as is, and preaches the Dharma clearly. Dōgen says in *Raihai tokuzui* that rocks and trees preach the Dharma, and that we can hear it preached by pillars, walls, and hedges. The Hua-yen master Fa-tsang said that 10,000 Buddhas preach the Dharma on the tip of a hair. Can we not also hear the Dharma in the Buddha's own words in the scriptures? Is the Buddha's body excluded from the scriptures? The Buddha is just as present in the scriptures as he is in formal zazen, and both have the power to help us realize our own Buddahood. This is true not only of the scriptures, but also of collections of koans, Hua-yen philosophy, and *Shōbōgenzō*. We may even think of these as bodhisattvas, in the same way that Tibetan Buddhists rightly think of their *tanka* paintings as bodhisattvas; not human bodhisattvas, to be sure, but bodhisattvas neverthe-less in their compassionate activity of filling us with faith and confidence, educating us, and inspiring us to see the truth which they embody and teach.

It is clear from *Nyorai zenshin* that for Dōgen the scriptures were both the voice of the Buddha and the Buddha himself, for he says that we pay homage to the Buddha when we pay homage to the sutra. As such, he says, we should "accept it, support it, read and recite it, explain, preach, and copy it, and in so doing become enlightened." Can we become enlightened in this way? Hui-neng became enlightened merely by hearing someone recite a portion of the *Diamond Sutra*. Hui-neng is not unique, for the records of Buddhist priests show that several were enlightened while reading the sutras, but admittedly, few achieve it in this manner. Something more is called for, and yet, having said this, it is worth mentioning that historically Buddhists have recognized the ability of intellectual study and understanding to eliminate some of our ignorance. Probably this kind of approach can only carry us so far in the direction of clarity of mind, but many bad ideas, prejudices, baseless assumptions, and other forms of ignorance can be removed simply by means of better information and calm, clear thinking. Thus, long before we see that things are empty (and are not even things) and become empty ourselves, a deep, meditative reading of a Buddhist text such as the *Diamond Sutra* can begin the process of learning to see that commonsense notions about reality and the actions which grow out of these notions are ignorant and mistaken. That may not be enlightenment, but it is something. It may be "only intellectual" understanding, but even mere intellectual understanding can begin to change our perspective, and that is what counts. I think that what Dōgen Zenji means is that reading the sutra is an important condition for our attainment of satori.

However, it is not only the sutra pages with their words in black print which are the whole body of the Buddha, for Dōgen Zenji tells us that reading and writing are themselves also the whole body of the Buddha. The point is, to repeat, that everything is the Buddha, nothing is excluded. It is, in other words, not just sitting in the meditation hall, wreathed with incense smoke, calm, passionless, and feeling spiritual, which is Buddha, but also reading, writing, copying, teaching, and paying homage to the scriptures. All our activities are Buddha activities, and this includes intellectual activity. Yes, thinking and reasoning are Buddha activity. Another way of looking at Zen practice is to see that its purpose is to free and activate the total individual, with all his talents, functions, and abilities, and this includes the mind as well as the feelings, the physical organism, and the will. And besides, it is a mistake to think that Zen considers any aspect of being as intrinsically evil, detrimental, or despicable. In fact, it is probably accurate to say that Buddhism, carefully considered, has never negated intellectual activity *per se*, but that it is only bad thinking and frivolous study and learning which are to be avoided. A person may very well feel insecure about his intellectual ability, or he may simply be too lazy to study and use his mind, but he should not make the mistake of believing that Zen supplies an ideological rationale for neglecting this aspect of his being.

The true goal of Buddhism is not mere self-spiritualization, but, as Dōgen Zenji says in *Hotsu bodai shin*, it is to save all sentient beings even before we ourselves are completely saved. Thus, service to others is the object of Zen practice. Our practice is a means of equipping us to be able to give effectively, which is to say, selflessly and without delusion. In commenting on the spiritual perfections *(pāramitā)*, Buddhist writers have often pointed out that the most essential of these is the first, which is giving *(dāna)*. Giving takes several forms, including material things (food, money, medicine, etc.) and the Dharma itself. But how can a person give the Dharma or try to save all beings if he is almost entirely ignorant of what the Dharma is? To give and serve implies first of all that we have something to give. Materially, we need only give what little we have, however small it is, and everyone has something. But to give the Dharma requires that we prepare ourselves in two ways: first, we must do zazen and make ourselves fit vessels for the Dharma; and second, we must learn the Buddhist tradition through reading and study and thereby have a Dharma to impart. In the Buddhist task of saving all sentient beings, Zen has no more need for fools and ignoramuses than does General Motors.

A good Buddhist practice would ideally combine zazen with a deep, careful study of Buddhist thought and practice. This has been the tradition of Tibetan Buddhism from its inception, and it has produced men who embodied (and still embody today in many lamas) the admirable fruits of both meditation and study. Looked at in one way, such study can be seen simply as an extension of practice, but at the same time, zazen and study complement and strengthen each other. Zazen experience enables the individual to have a much deeper understanding of doctrines than if study were pursued without the formal meditation, and at the same time, a deep understanding and appreciation for the beauty, subtlety, and power of Buddhist teachings can help to guide, strengthen, and inspire one's zazen practice. Christian theologians have traditionally warned about a simple faith which is not supported by reason, saying that reason without faith is arrogant and shallow, but faith without reason is blind. Blindless is to be avoided at all costs, and in Buddhism also, which stresses seeing and being truly awake, blindness is no virtue. In pursuing zazen practice and learning to see and be aware, we need all the help we can get. This help comes from many directions, but one of the best sources, and one which is always available, is scriptural literature or any other literature which strengthens and guides the rest of our practice.

# NOTES

1.  R. H. Blyth, *Buddhist Sermons on Christian Texts* (Tokyo: Kokudosha, 1952), p. 31.

# SIX

*Giving Life to Our Lives*

We really have nothing but our present lives here and now as we live them from moment to moment. The past is gone as an actuality, and exists, if at all, only as memory and condition. The future does not exist at all, except as potentiality and possibility. The prospect of future lives in remote heavens as a compensation for the inadequacy of our present lives is a bad tradeoff for losing out on the present. Even if literal rebirth or reincarnation is a fact, we certainly shall not reappear in this world in the form we possess now, for we shall be other selves, with no recollection of what we were previously. And even in this present life, there are no better places to be than where we are right now, and if this present place and situation are vexing to the spirit, the problem is within ourselves, not with the place or situation. We must face what seems to be a stubborn fact, that all we can be sure of as a reality is this present life, in some particular place, involved in particular events.

Various philosophies have recognized this fact and have responded to it in their own ways. Lieh-tzu, a Taoist, realizing that he had but this one life to live with no hope of another, concluded that one could do no better than live life to the fullest, indulging oneself fully in good food, good wine, and all the other pleasures of life. His was the hedonistic approach to life. Hedonism is the confession of despair and meaninglessness, and it has been advocated by many, including some of the early Greek philosophers. In the West in the last several generations, where true religious faith has almost completely deteriorated, it is evident that many people have eagerly embraced hedonism in despair of any greater purpose or meaning in life.

However, there are other ways of responding to the fact that we are stuck in the here and now. The Zen of Dōgen Zenji is a way of dealing satisfactorily with the fact that we find ourselves, always, in a certain time, in a certain body, living a certain kind of life along with other lives. And Dōgen tells us, in words that sound like those of the hedonist, to live life fully, to give life to our lives, and not to live dead lives. But Dōgen's counsel is diametrically opposed to the attitude of the hedonist, who would flinch were he to read such essays from *Shōbōgenzō* as *Gyōji* ("Continuous Practice") and *Kajō* ("Daily Life"). The hedonist has a very acute sense of what has value in terms of making life supremely pleasant and entertaining for him. He must always be in certain kinds of places and avoid others. Leisure and entertainment are preferable to any kind of work or effort. Certain kinds of people are pleasant to associate with, others not. Only the best of everything will do, never the common or the cheap. The hedonist would diligently shun the life of the Zen patriarchs, which, Dōgen tells us, is nothing more than drinking tea and eating rice. Both the hedonist and the Zen patriarch are struck with the facticity of the here and now, but whereas the Zen patriarch gives life to all events and enters them completely and without reservation, the hedonist studiously avoids certain events and strives to manage his life in such a way that he only enters fully, if ever, into those situations which he has prejudged as worthwhile.

The everyday life of the Zen patriarch consists merely of eating rice and drinking tea. This "eating rice and drinking tea" has a very deep meaning in the final analysis; one thing it means is that an enlightened individual is one who has learned not to kill ordinary acts such as eating plain rice or drinking plain tea. "Eating rice and drinking tea" means, of course, ordinary, everyday life, and consequently not to kill these acts means not to kill our ordinary, everyday lives. There are two ways we can kill them. First, we can kill them by living them in a semi-stupor, in unawareness, mechanically, stupidly, as if we were drugged. Second, we can kill them by discriminating, devaluating and demeaning, which occurs when we actively prefer other situations which we consider more valuable. To yearn for lobster and fine wine while having plain rice and tea is to discriminate against the rice and tea, which demeans and kills them. To want to be in some other place is to kill this place. To want to be entertained instead of painting the garage is to kill work. This killing is the opposite of giving life to these things, for giving life is nothing more than understanding that what we are, what we do, and where we do it is good enough. They are more than good enough; they are perfect. Our problem is that we kill so much of our lives in the expectation that there is something better someplace else. This is delusion.

Bashō has a *haiku* which simply says,

> Lice, fleas,
> The horse pissing
> Beside my pillow.

He had been wandering about Japan, as he liked to do, and found himself at nightfall with no place to spend the night except in a shelter for horses. As he tried to sleep, he felt lice and fleas begin to crawl over him and heard (and perhaps felt also) the nearby horse relieve itself. Notice what the poem does not contain. It does not contain self-pity, anger, disgust, or irritation. There is, in fact, no judgement at all, and even the poet himself is absent from the poem, for the event has no personal meaning for Bashō. He merely reports what is and presumably goes to sleep. This ability to enter into the moment completely, without judgement, without condemnation of the present and yearning for a nonexistent alternative is somewhat akin to the daily lives of the patriarchs, who just eat rice and drink tea. In the plain rice and tea, and also, one suspects, in the situation in the horse shelter, there is some understanding of what those events really are, an appreciation of a deeper meaning of the events which eludes most of us.

Giving life to our lives therefore does not mean that we insist, as the hedonist does, that we must always be "happy," gratified, entertained, or self-fulfilled. Rather, giving life to our lives means coming to understand that one place is really as good as another, and the pattern of our lives is good enough. It is knowing that there are no "best places," "best occupation," and so on. It also means thoroughly growing up, becoming an adult fully in the sense that life does not have to be organized in terms of fun and excitement. It also means becoming serious, because one is able to see that life has meaning that extends far beyond the confines of self-interest.

However, we do not learn these things easily or naturally, and so we have to learn them through arduous training. Without this training, we continue all our lives to kill and kill and kill, until our lives are frantic, tormented, and insane. I have written about this kind of training in earlier chapters, and all the chapters of *Shōbōgenzō* which I have translated in the following pages tell us how to train in such a way that we give life to our lives. *Kajō* ("Daily Life") tells us that to live our lives as the constant actualization of our inherent enlightenment is simply to eat rice and drink tea. Doesn't everyone do this? I mean eat, sleep, work, play, pay the taxes, shop for groceries, talk with a friend, and all the rest. We do in a way, of course, but we do not do these things in the manner that makes all the difference. While we are eating plain rice, our minds are filled with longing to be elsewhere eating finer food, and so we hardly ever really just eat rice or drink tea as the Zen patriarchs do, because for us the rice and tea are just not good enough.

In short, we do not live each "now" single-mindedly. We all know what single-mindedness is, for at times we do live with a single mind. When we are pursuing a loved one, when we are faced with an opponent in fighting, we are single-minded in the way a cat is single-minded when stalking a bird. Then there is nothing but this one reality, and our minds are cleared of phantasy, resentment, longing, and so on. We are totally involved in the most active way with the present circumstance. Buddhist literature uses the word *eka-citta* (Japanese: *isshin*), which literally means "one mind," or, as we would say, "single-minded." To do anything with one mind, single-mindedly, is to become totally absorbed in whatever we are doing, so that when we do zazen we do nothing but zazen, and when we drink tea, we just drink tea. It sounds very easy, and in a way it is, but in fact we can't do it easily without training. The Japanese have a saying: "You can't chase two rabbits at the same time." If you try to catch both rabbits, you lose them both. In the same way, if your mind is elsewhere while you try to do zazen, you lose the present zazen, and it goes without saying that you do not possess the phantasy either. If while drinking plain water you yearn for beer, both the beer and the water are lost. The question is, When will we ever live our real life, which is always the present, the "now" where we always find ourselves? We can lose a whole lifetime by dwelling on where we were in the past or where we wish to be in the future.

What must it be like to be enlightened? We imagine that it involves spectacular feats such as levitation, or walking on water, or reading the minds of others. Or we may imagine some kind of transformation into a saintly figure draped in flowing robes, emitting an aura, uttering holy platitudes, and swaying entire crowds with solemn, authoritative pronouncements of the Truth. Yet Dōgen Zenji says that it is just eating rice and drinking tea. But this simple act is indeed marvellous, far beyond the capabilities of the vast majority of people.

Yün-yen (Ungan) and Tao-wu (Dōgo), two Zen monks, were talking one day, and Yün-yen asked Tao-wu, "Why does Kuan-yin [Avalokiteśvara] have so many hands and eyes?" Yün-yen was referring to the images of Avalokiteśvara which have many hands and eyes. Tao-wu replied, "It is like a person who gropes behind himself in the night, searching for his pillow." "I understand! I understand!" said Yün-yen. "What do you understand?" Tao-wu asked. Said Yün-yen, "The whole body is covered with hands and eyes." "Not bad, not bad," said Tao-wu, "you have expressed it pretty well." "That's as well as I can do," said Yün-yen. "How about you, elder brother?" Tao-wu replied, "The whole body is hands and eyes." (*Shōbōgenzō Kannon*)

Tao-wu's answer is marvellous, and it is no surprise that he became the Dharma heir of Yüeh-shan (Yakusan) in the lineage of Ch'ing-yüan Hsing-ssu (Seigen Gyōshi) and Shiht'ou Hsi-chien (Sekitō Kisen). The answer to the question of what it means to live the enlightened life is evident in Taowu's statement. The images of Avalokiteśvara with their many arms and many heads and eyes are the result of a brilliant attempt by artists to portray in clear iconographical style the essence of enlightenment, which is dynamic activity guided by understanding or insight (i.e., "seeing into"). The object was to symbolize compassionate activity, and the many arms and hands might have been countless, had this been artistically possible. The point is that Avalokiteśvara personifies absolute, unqualified, compassionate activity, and what better way to portray this than by giving him so many arms and hands? The activity is so complete that we cannot even speak of Avalokiteśvara and his activity, as if there were two realities. Avalokiteśvara *is* compassionate activity, he is *just* hands and eyes.

But such compassionate activity is not possible in the absence of a penetrating insight into the nature of existence. The ordinary person, controlled by passion, sentimentality, and, ultimately, self-interest, fails to be truly compassionate. This is because he is deluded and does not understand who he is, who the other is, or the nature of the relationship between the two. When his eyes are really open, when he can clearly see by means of prajñā insight, then whatever he does will be truly compassionate. The many eyes of Avalokiteśvara clearly express this seeing. Thus, just as he is nothing but hands and arms, so is he also nothing but eyes, for he is in reality the embodiment of the perfect union of insight and compassion, activity illuminated by understanding.

It is said that Avalokiteśvara appears in the world in countless forms. Doesn't this mean that there are countless Avalokiteśvaras, that any individual who is able to act compassionately through his insight is Avalokiteśvara? Sometimes we are being the Avalokiteśvara we really are, and sometimes we are not. When we are not being Avalokiteśvara, we indeed have only two hands and two eyes. Sometimes, in fact, we have only one hand and one eye. Then we do not eat our plain food and drink our plain tea in the way that the Zen patriarchs did.

When Dōgen Zenji says that the daily life of the patriarchs is nothing but eating rice and drinking tea, he means that their actions around the monastery are no different from those of any other person. Yet their eating rice is not at all like ours because ours is not illuminated by understanding. However, it is not only a matter of seeing and understanding. The act itself must be a total act, an act performed not merely with one or two hands, or even a hundred or a million hands, but with an infinity of hands. It is an act performed by one who is just hands. Such an act, even so ordinary a one as eating, is performed with total exertion, without omitting even a fragment of one's being from the act. This is what Dōgen means by *gūjin*, which I discussed briefly in a previous chapter. *Gūjin* is the performance of any act in total commitment and absorption. It is also action performed in the knowledge that the act or situation is the total manifestation of reality. It is to act as the Avalokiteśvara we really are.

What Dōgen Zenji and other Zen patriarchs taught, then, is drinking tea with the body which is all hands and eyes. It is, in the end, no more than this. Zen literature is almost devoid of supernatural objectives and values. No one seems ever to have wished to be like a god, to have paranormal powers, or even to be saintly. In fact, the Zen masters have always been distinctly unsaintly. There seems to be plenty of evidence, on the contrary, that the object was to gain the ability to live an ordinary life illumined by understanding, which is very human and very humanistic. Dōgen Zenji expresses this vision in terms of "eating rice and drinking tea."

The essay called *Gyōji* ("Continuous Practice") is a long description of the daily lives of the patriarchal masters from the time of Śākyamuni almost down to the time of Dōgen himself. These stories are almost completely devoid of the saintly, the miraculous, or the supernatural. Instead, it is very clear that all these men led ordinary, though active and creative, lives. Story after story is much the same: each master, when he himself was a student, studied with his own master, eventually realized his own awakened nature, and continued for the rest of his life to manifest this awakening in all his daily actions. Lin-chi planted cedars for the benefit of future generations, Ta-an ate rice and "raised an ox," and Pai-chang worked in the fields with his students well into old age, saying, "A day without working, a day without eating."

Dōgen Zenji calls this activity *gyōji*. *Gyō* is activity, performance, and training. It is not just any activity but activity illumined by understanding. *Ji* means "to maintain," "to hold on to." *Gyōji* is thus activity in which we constantly make a strong effort to see and live our daily lives in the special way which constitutes Zen training. It is not merely being constantly busy as a result of some puritanical sense of the sinfulness of idleness. Nor is it a life of frenetic activity which is oriented towards the accomplishment of grand objectives. It is just eating, drinking, working, sleeping, and in general carrying on with one's ordinary life. It is life as continuous training. It is thus the life of desirelessness, without preferences, without picking and choosing. It is thus also the life of emptiness. To be empty is to be content with what one is, where one is, and with what one must do. Consequently, one lives life always here, in this place, now, and in this particular way, entering totally into each act without reservations or conditions, always actualizing, realizing, and giving life to all these simple beads of experience we call "now." This *gyōji*, consequently, is none other than living life with the thousand hands and eyes of Avalokiteśvara. In fact, says Dōgen, this is such a total activity that the Avalokiteśvara of Yün-yen and Tao-wu has countless hands and eyes. This activity, this practice, is galaxies away from the activity of two hands and eyes, of one hand and one eye, or, as is unfortunately usually the case, of one hand and no eyes at all.

Dōgen Zenji says in *Gyōji* that continuous practice is always now, for the nature of continuous practice is such that it cannot exist either in the past or in the future. To practice continuously means to be constantly actualizing our enlightened nature anew in each event, and we cannot do this if our minds dwell in the past or future. To be in the past or future mentally while we are physically in the present means that there is a dividedness in our lives, a lack of complete centeredness. Memory and phantasy *per se* are harmless, but a very real problem arises in our lives when we do not completely occupy the reality which is the present, which is all we will ever really have. This is how we kill our lives. But "now" and "continuous practice" are one and the same thing; when we are engaged in continuous practice, we are totally immersed in "now"; when we totally immerse ourselves in the actuality of present circumstances, which means to see them and experience them as Avalokiteśvara, we are engaged in continuous practice. Thus Dōgen Zenji says that this "now" did not exist within us in the past in seedform, nor is it the case that first we engage in continuous practice and then "now" is manifested, but when the one exists, the other exists also for the first time.

What is this "now"? It is not really the "now" of time, which is the sliver-thin juncture between the past and future, although it may be helpful to think of "now" in that way. If "now" is the pure immediacy of lived experience in each event, then each "now" is doomed to cease and become memory, to be replaced by an entirely new "now," and this process goes on forever. In this sense, there is a stream of "nows," one following the other, but experientially they are not lived as units of time, as a present standing between past and future, but rather as just totally-lived beads of experience. But the point is, the totally-lived experience of one "now" does not guarantee that the next moment will also be totally lived in the same fashion. Consequently, to be engaged in continuous practice necessitates a constant effort to awaken again, over and over, as each new experience arises. Continuous practice is therefore a process of actualizing our inherent Buddhahood anew in each occasion in our daily life. There is no resting on our laurels. We must empty ourselves anew, over and over, and this is continuous practice, and it is the real "now."

The whole universe is an ocean of dazzling light. So says a line in the memorial service *(gakki)* recited in the Dharma hall on the occasion of remembering and honoring our spiritual ancestors. We need to proceed in our practice in the faith that the whole universe is indeed an ocean of dazzling light, the very body of the Buddha. We need also to proceed in the faith that if we practice with the urgency of someone trying to extinguish a flame in his hair, we will in time come to *see* that the whole universe is an ocean of dazzling light. For purposes of our practice, it is important to remember that it is the whole universe which is an ocean of dazzling light, not just half the universe or the rather meager portion we have habitually come to associate with light. This means we can find that light everywhere, in every event, in every new "now" as it unfolds and becomes an actuality. None of these "nows" is deficient in light, no matter how deficient or terrible, ordinary or dull they may appear. Eating plain rice and drinking tea are part of this ocean of dazzling light. The task of the individual who trains in Zen is to learn to see this, for Zen practice is no more and no less than this.

How ordinary, plain and simple Zen is! It is a life with one's feet on the ground of one's native home, toes buried in the fragrant dirt. It is a life of appreciation for the wonderful taste of plain boiled rice and green tea. It is a life of constantly bowing to the Buddha whose face is seen shining from every entity, every event. Of course, this life is not enough for everyone, and so the world is a noisy arena of struggle and competition, envy, frustration, and insatiable desire for more and better. Plain rice and tea are not enough for us. Someplace else, in a future time, we expect to find thorough satisfaction in comfort, security, power, and pleasure. Will we ever find it? Is it worth the price? Is there really anything better than plain rice and tea?

# SEVEN

*Concerning the Translation*

It is customary for translators of Dōgen Zenji's writings to say something about how difficult it is to translate his works into another language and to modestly disclaim any hopes for a perfect translation. I would like to take this opportunity to join them. I believe that I have succeeded by and large in being accurate and that with the possible exception of a few places, I have not made Dōgen Zenji say something in English which he never said in Japanese. The reader may therefore proceed in the confidence that the following pages represent the original Japanese to a fairly reasonable degree, but undoubtedly they are not perfect.

The truth of the matter is that Dōgen's writings are very difficult, even for a person who reads Japanese with some ease. Even most Japanese who write about Dōgen admit that his writing is very difficult. How much more difficult is it for any Westerner who only learned Japanese later in life on the college or graduate level and who came to Dōgen's writings at an even later date.

There are several reasons why this literature is so difficult. First, the literary form of Japanese has changed considerably since the time of Dōgen. Expressions current in the thirteenth century have completely dropped out of usage, the meaning of other terms has changed, and there is less of a tendency now to incorporate lengthy Chinese phrases into a Japanese sentence. Dōgen wrote in Japanese, but frequently he incorporated whole sentences or more extended passages in Sung Chinese, with its own syntax, without the particles that make the Japanese clearer, into a passage which is otherwise Japanese. Also, he tended to leave out particles such as *wa, ga* and *o* even when writing Japanese, a custom of his time but one which sometimes makes a sentence difficult to construe grammatically. Low-class, colloquial expressions, of which the Chinese masters were fond, abound in *Shōbōgenzō*, and their meaning can often be found only after consulting special dictionaries and glossaries. Some are not even recorded.

These expressions are also difficult to translate exactly and smoothly into English, and while I have tried to arrive at a translation which is as close to the original as I could make it, at times a term, a phrase, or a whole sentence had to be paraphrased. In these cases, literal translation is not possible, and the best a translator can hope for is a sense of the original. Let me illustrate what I mean. A Japanese sentence such as *itonamu koto nakare* can be exactly translated without paraphrase or loss of literalism as "Do not do it." But consider the term *zushin bishin*, which occurs in the *Kannon* chapter of *Shōbōgenzō: zu* means "head," *bi* means "tail," and *shin* here means "correct," "upright," "perfect," "true," "orthodox," and "straight." The terms thus literally mean something like "head perfect, tail perfect." But the sentence in which it occurs would then literally read, "Are they [one's own hands and eyes] merely one or two pieces of the head perfect tail perfect hands and eyes?" On the other hand, if one consults several dictionaries, this old term is said to mean "from beginning to end," or "perfect from start to finish." But this does not seem to fit into the sentence either. After considerable study and research, a comparison of contexts for the same expression, and so on, one discovers that it means something like "absolute." Thus, what Dōgen is asking is whether one's own hands and eyes are merely one or two pieces of the absolute, or absolutely manifested, hands and eyes of Avalokiteśvara Bodhisattva. And in context, this makes sense. My point is twofold: first, the text of *Shōbōgenzō* is extremely difficult for any translator. Second, despite a sustained attempt to keep as literally close to Dōgen's own manner of expression as possible, sometimes a paraphrase or otherwise nonliteral rendition is required and is inescapable if the English version is to make any sense at all.

Another difficulty arises from the fact that *Shōbōgenzō* is a Zen text, and I doubt that any other religious literature (with the possible exception of Sufi literature, with which I am not all that familiar) is quite like it. Zen writers usually do not express themselves in the conventional, everyday language of society. First, their language tends to be very concrete instead of abstract. People generally use a highly abstract level of discourse, so that we all tend to sound like metaphysicians compared with the Zen masters. Thus, when asked "What is the Buddha?", a Zen master will reply, "The cypress tree in the courtyard," instead of involving you in a very abstract discussion about such things as "immanence," "absolute," "reality," "emptiness," "truth," and so on. Also, they do not see things the way common folk do, so that their behavior and expression are unconventional and unpredictable, which creates another problem for the translator. Even after individual words and phrases are deciphered and the syntax is solved, the resulting English sentence is frequently so bizarre that the translator cannot be sure that the translation is correct. Confidence comes only with some degree of familiarity with the special world of Zen literature.

A related problem in the translation of *Shōbōgenzō* concerns the fact that Dōgen Zenji himself was not an ordinary man, as careful study of his writings will make clear. He addresses the reader from a level of spiritual insight that is greatly superior to ours, and the reader's challenge is to try to comprehend Dōgen's vision of reality from the vantage point of his remarkable achievement. He is very difficult to follow because he sees a reality we do not even vaguely imagine. This is a real problem for the translator because no matter how learned he or she is in reading ancient Chinese and Japanese texts, understanding complex Buddhist doctrines, the history of Buddhism, and the like, the point of a passage will sometimes be missed because strictly speaking the translator does not really understand what Dōgen is saying.

This problem is further deepened by the fact that Dōgen Zenji was among other things a poet with a deep sensitivity to language. He used words carefully and precisely, and consequently the nuances of words are very important. The translator must struggle to find as exact an equivalent to Dōgen's terminology as is possible. When these nuances are obliterated by a general paraphrase of the original, something has been lost which is crucial to the text. This is particularly true, for instance, in the great many instances in which Dōgen carefully discusses the terminology of some koan.

Another problem is related to the fact that Dōgen Zenji spoke authoritatively about life from the standpoint of an enlightened man. Because he saw reality in a certain way and was utterly convinced of the validity of his vision, he tended to make conventional language and traditional Buddhist literature serve this vision in a most original and striking way. A well-known example is his reading of the passage in the *Mahāpāranirvāna Sūtra* which says, "All sentient beings possess Buddha-nature." Convinced as he was that there are not two separate realities, beings and Buddha, but rather that all things, including nonsentient beings, are Buddha just as they are, he reads the passage as saying, "All existence *is* Buddha-nature." Throughout *Shōbōgenzō*, language is made to serve the truth as he saw it.

Thus, translating *Shōbōgenzō* is a difficult task. It is my belief that the ideal translator of this literature would be a person who knew thirteenth century Japanese well, was sensitive to language in general, particularly his own, was well trained in the history, practices, and doctrines of Buddhism, and approached the text in the light of his own Zen practice. I feel that this last requirement is very important, because unless the translator has some insight, however small, into what Dōgen Zenji is saying, he will miss much in the text and the translation will suffer.

I also believe that despite all the difficulties of *Shōbōgenzō*, it is possible to translate it in such a way that the considerable power and beauty of the original can be retained. I agree that in some instances only a paraphrase is possible, but for the most part the English version can faithfully reflect the original without lapsing into pidgin English or gibberish. I have tried to keep this in mind at all times while translating the text, for it is my feeling that *Shōbōgenzō* is one of the most remarkable pieces of world literature and as such deserves all the care and attention one can direct to it.

A few words about procedures. First, I have written Chinese personal and place names in the Chinese pronunciation instead of in the more familiar Japanese pronunciation by which they are usually known. As a result of this, the reader will find "Hui-neng" instead of the more familiar "Enō," "Huang-po" instead of "Obaku," and so on. If the Chinese names themselves are translations or transliterations of Indian names, I have restored the name to the Indian original. Thus, the reader will find "Avalokiteśvara" instead of "Kuan-yin" (or the Japanese "Kannon"), and so on. Also, where in some instances only the Japanese name is widely known and when I have felt that identification was important, I have added the more familiar Japanese pronunciation in parentheses after the Chinese name. An example is Shih-t'ou

(Sekitō). The geneology chart at the back of the book will further clarify these correspondences. Furthermore, I have used essential diacritical marks for all words that require them, since these indicate pronunciation features which are intrinsic to the words. Thus, *nirvāna, samsāra, Śākyamuni, Sekitō, Dōgen,* and many other Sanskrit, Chinese, and Japanese words.

These translations could not have been done without the help of Japanese scholars whose reference works and translations of Dōgen's writings into modern Japanese have helped me at every step of the way. Some of the more important works are listed below, and I recommend them to anyone who attempts to translate *Shōbōgenzō*.

1. *Shōbōgenzō shisō taikei,* by Okada Gihō. Modern Japanese translation with commentary.
2. *Shōbōgenzō sankyū,* by Yasutani Hakuun Roshi. Invaluable and illuminating commentary by a contemporary Zen master.
3. *Zenyaku shōbōgenzō,* by Nakamura Sōichi. Very good translation of *Shōbōgenzō* into modern Japanese. His dictionary of expressions in *Shōbōgenzō,* the *Shōbōgenzō yōgo jiten,* has been indispensible.
4. *Shōbōgenzō chūkai zensho,* by Jimbo Nyoten and Andō Bun'ei. A collection of some of the best known and most authoritative older commentaries on *Shōbōgenzō*.

I have also benefited from other Western translations, particularly the following.

1. *Dōgen Kigen: Mystical Realist,* by Hee-jin Kim.
2. *Zen Master Dōgen,* by Yūhō Yokoi and Daizen Victoria.
3. Various chapters of *Shōbōgenzō,* translated by Abe Masao and Norman Waddell, which have appeared in recent issues of the journal *Eastern Buddhist.*
4. Several translations on which I have collaborated with Taizan Maezumi Roshi of the Zen Center of Los Angeles

do not appear in this volume but will appear in future issues of the Zen Writings Series, published by the Zen Center.

# TRANSLATIONS

# FUKAN ZAZENGI

*"General Recommendations for Doing Zazen"*

The Way is essentially perfect and exists everywhere. There is no need either to seek or to realize the Way. The Truth which carries us along is sovereign and does not require our efforts. Need I say that it excels this world? Who can believe that the expedient of [mirror-]wiping is necessary?[1] Essentially the Truth is very close to you; is it then necessary to run around in search of it?

Even so, if there is the slightest error, there is a gulf as great as that between heaven and earth. If so much as a thought of agreeable or disagreeable arises, one becomes confused. For instance, you may feel proud in your comprehension, or you may feel prosperous in achieving satori. Even if you acquire satori in the blink of an eye, acquire the Way and enlighten your mind, feel as if you could assault heaven itself, and charge into the Dharma as if on a mere saunter, you may shortly lose the way of dropping off the body.

How may one [now] perceive the traces of that one of

Jetavana [the Buddha], who saw all things as they truly are with his own enlightened nature and yet still did zazen for six years? The fame of that one of Shao-lin Temple [Bodhidharma] who transmitted the mind-seal [from India] and who for nine years still sat facing a wall [in meditation] is being transmitted even now. If this was true of the ancient worthies, people of today must also exert themselves.

For this reason, you must suspend your attempts to understand by means of scrutinizing words, reverse the activity of the mind which seeks externally, and illuminate your own true nature. Mind and body will fall off spontaneously, and your original face will be revealed. If you wish to achieve such a thing, you must exert yourself in this matter at once.

For zazen, you will need a quiet room. Eat and drink in moderation. Forget about the concerns of the day and leave such matters alone. Do not judge things as good or evil, and cease such distinctions as "is" and "is not." Halt the flow of the mind, and cease conceptualizing, thinking, and observing. Don't sit in order to become a Buddha, because becoming a Buddha has nothing to do with such things as sitting or lying down.

In the room which you use for zazen, spread some thick mats and place a firm, round pillow on them. Sit on the pillow with your legs crossed either in the full lotus position or (sit) in the half lotus position. This means [in the full lotus position] that you place your right foot on your left thigh, and your left foot on your right thigh. In the half lotus position, you just put your left foot on your right thigh [with the right foot on the mat beneath your left thigh].

Loosen your clothes and belt and arrange them neatly. Next, place your right hand [palm up] on top of your left foot, and place your left hand [palm up] in the palm of your right hand. Both thumb tips should touch slightly.

Now regulate your posture so you are sitting properly, leaning neither to the left nor to the right, forward nor backward. [Looked at from the side], your ears and shoulders should be in a straight line, and from the front, your nose will be in a direct line with your navel. Place your tongue against the roof of your mouth, and keep your teeth and lips closed. Your eyes should be [slightly] open, and your breathing should be soft.

When your body posture is correct, breathe in and out [once, deeply]. Sway left and right [several times] and then sit firmly and resolutely. Think about the unthinkable. How do you think about the unthinkable? Do not think. These are the essentials of zazen.

That which we call zazen is not a way of developing concentration. It is simply the comfortable way. It is practice which measures your satori to the fullest, and is in fact satori itself. It is the manifestation of the ultimate reality, and in it you will no longer be trapped as in a basket or a cage. If you understand my meaning [and do zazen correctly], you will be like a dragon who has reached the water, or like a tiger who trusts in the mountain where he dwells. Know that the true Dharma itself is present [there in zazen], and that confusion and distraction are eradicated right from the beginning.

When you get up from zazen, move quietly and slowly. Do not make violent movements. When we contemplate the past, we observe that transcending both the sacred and the profane, or such things as dying while in zazen or while standing [which the old Zen masters did] came about through this power. It is even more difficult to explain with words and analysis how the ancient masters could seize upon the crucial moment which brought about satori in a disciple by pointing a finger, using the tip of a pole, a needle, or a mallet, and give encouragement with the *hossu*,[2] a fist, a stick or a shout. How can supernatural powers explain practice and enlightenment? Practice and enlightenment are the majestic deportment of the body, beyond the sights and sounds [of this world]. What can they be other than the Dharma which is prior to understanding and analysis?

Such being the case, there is no question here at all of

being intelligent or stupid, nor is there any difference between the quickwitted and the dull. If you exert yourself single-mindedly, this is practicing the Way itself. Practice and realization leave not a trace of impurity, and the person who advances in the Way is an ordinary person.

This world or other worlds, India or China, all equally preserve the seal of the Buddha.[3] He who adheres exclusively to the customs of Zen practices zazen only, doing nothing but sitting resolutely on the ground. You may hear of ten thousand distinctions or a thousand differences,[4] but just do zazen earnestly and make an effort in the Way. You don't need to abandon your own sitting place and just for the amusement of it go to some other country. If you err by a single step, you lose the Way.

Now you have acquired the essential, which is a human form. Do not pass over from the light to the shadow [by pursuing other matters]. Take care of this essential instrument of the Buddha's Way. Could you really be content with a spark from a stone [when the blazing sun is shining]? And that is not all; your body is like dew on the grass, your life is as brief as a flash of lightening. Momentary and vain, it is lost in an instant.

I entreat you who practice in the splendid tradition of Zen, do not grope around as if you were in a group of blind people [trying to determine what an elephant is] or be in doubt when you see a real dragon [instead of false ones].[5] Just persevere in the simple Way which has been indicated for you so directly. Value those beings who have perfected their own practice and have finished what was to be done. If you conform to the satori of all the Buddhas, you will become an heir to the samādhi of all the [Zen] patriarchs. If you practice like this for a long time, you will surely become like them. The precious treasury will open its doors all by itself, and the treasure will be yours to use as you wish.

# NOTES

1. An allusion to the methods of the so-called Northern school of Zen taught by Shen-hsiu, competitor with Hui-neng for the title of sixth patriarch. The mind was conceived as being like a bright mirror which reflects everything as long as it is kept immaculate, which is to say, free of discriminating thought. Hui-neng said that there is no mirror and therefore nothing to be defiled.

2. A *hossu* is a whisk made of horse or yak tail hairs and was carried as a symbol of rank. The raising or lowering of the *hossu* was often used by Zen masters as a teaching device, as were all the other devices such as shouting, hitting, and so on.

3. The seal of the Buddha is Buddha-mind, which is transmitted by the Zen tradition.

4. These are different methods of meditation or different methods of training in general.

5. There is a very old story of several blind men examining an elephant by touch and trying to decide what the elephant is like. Because each touches only one part of the elephant, each has a partial and therefore inadequate idea of what an elephant is. The second reference is to a famous artist who specialized in painting dragons. One day a real dragon flew into his room and the artist did not know what it was.

# KEISEI SANSHOKU

*"The Sounds of Valley Streams, the Forms of the Mountains"*

Many are the Buddha patriarchs who have transmitted the supreme Way to the highest enlightenment and who have taught the methods of practice. The traces still remain of our predecessors who broke their bones in learning the Way. You should study the life of the second patriarch Hui-k'o, who cut off his arm in order to receive the teaching, and do not be attached to even a single hair of your body.[1] When you finally achieve the various liberations by doing zazen, everything that was withheld from you in the past because of your discriminating mind will be revealed to you at once. This instant of revelation of reality, I do not understand it, nor do you, nor does anyone else. Not even the Buddha vision sees it, so how can it be fathomed by human calculation?

There once lived a Chinese *upāsaka* named [Su] Tung-p'o (Sotōba),[2] whose family name was Su and whose official name was Shih. His courtesy name was Tzu-chan. He was very famous, a real dragon in the ocean of letters, and he studied the dragons and *nāgas* in the ocean of Buddhism. He sported freely in the depths [like a dragon] and rose up to the high-piled clouds. Once, on Mount Lu, <u>he was enlightened when he heard the sound of valley streams flowing in the night.</u> He composed a verse and presented it to Ch'an master Ch'ang-Tsung, and it said,

> The sounds of the valley streams are His
>     long, broad tongue;
> The forms of the mountains are His pure
>     body.
> At night I heard the myriad sutra-verses
>     uttered
> How can I relate to others what they say?

When he presented this verse to Master Tsung, the master approved it. He was the Ch'an master Chao-hsüeh Ch'ang-tsung, who was the Dharma heir of Ch'an master Huang-lung Hui-nan. Hui-nan himself was the Dharma heir of the Ch'an master Tz'u-ming Ch'u-yüan. Later, this upasaka met the Ch'an master Fa-in (Liao-yuan) and at that time Fa-in gave him the precepts and robes. Thereafter, the upasaka always put on the robes and did zazen. He respectfully presented Fa-in with a sash decorated with priceless jewels. People of that time said, "This sort of thing is not possible for ordinary people like us to do, he must be very unusual."

This being the case, can we now not consider the circumstances of Su Tung-p'o's hearing the valley streams and becoming enlightened to be a great benefit extending down to the present time? It is deplorable, but it is almost as if something were lacking in people's ability to understand the expounding of the Dharma in these boundless manifestations of the Buddha's body. If this revelation of the Buddha's body is the preaching of the Dharma, then how are people today to see the forms of the mountains and hear the sound of the streams? Do they hear them as a single phrase? Are they just half a phrase? Are they a myriad verses? How regrettable it is that there are sounds and forms in the streams and mountains that we can not understand. Yet it is a matter for delight that we have the opportunity to acquire the proper conditions for experiencing the Way in these sounds and forms. The sounds are never stilled, and the forms never cease to exist. This being so, does this mean that when they are revealed the body is near and that when they are obscured the body is not near? Is it the whole body, or is it just half the body? Because the springs and autumns of former times have completely become mountains and streams, you cannot detect them in mountains and streams; because the times prior to this night have completely become mountains and streams, you can see them as mountains and streams. Today's bodhisattva who practices the Way should begin his study of the Way in the knowledge that the mountains flow and the stream does not flow.

As for that night when Su Tung-p'o was enlightened, he had on the previous day asked Master Tsung about the saying that even insentient things preach the Dharma, and while he had had no really significant experience from hearing the master's explanation, when later that night he heard the sounds of the streams, it was as if the billowing waves touched the high heavens. When this occurred, the sound astonished the upasaka, but should we say it was the sounds of the streams, or should we rather say that it was the sound of Master Chao-hsüeh flowing? Perhaps Chao-hsüeh's discussion of the idea of insentient things preaching the Dharma had not really stopped, but was imperceptibly mixed with the night sounds of the valley streams. Now, someone will say that it was "a single water," or that it was the "ocean of oneness," the oneness of the water of the Dharma and the water of the streams. If we examine the matter closely, was it the upāsaka who became enlightened, or was it the mountains and streams which became enlightened? If anyone has eyes to see, then certainly anyone is able to see the long, broad tongue and the pure body.

Again, when the Ch'an master Hsiang-yen Chih-hsien was practicing the Way under Ch'an master Ta-wei Ta-yüan, Ta-wei said to him, "You are quite bright and seem to understand everything. Without any reliance on your learned treatises, from what you were before your parents conceived you, give me one single phrase concerning the Way." Try as he might, Hsiang-yen could think of nothing to say in reply. He regretted his mind and body, and try as he might to find some clue in the books he had accumulated over many years, it was no use at all. So he set fire to all his precious books, saying, "Rice cakes in a picture do not satisfy one's hunger. I will no longer seek the Buddha Way in this present life, and my practice will be that of serving the rice to practicing monks." So saying, he spent many years serving meals to the monks. The expression, "meal-serving monk" refers to someone who serves rice and other food to the monks who are practicing. It is like carrying the trays of food for the nobility, or like the position of waiter in our country.

One day, he spoke to Ta-wei: "My mind is clouded and I cannot speak; say something that will help me, Chief Priest!" Ta-wei replied, "Unfortunately, I cannot say anything for you. Maybe later you would resent my having done so." So the years passed, and Hsiang-yen travelled to Wu-tang Mountain searching for the whereabouts of the national teacher, Ta-cheng, and near the hermitage of the national teacher he built a grass hut, which he used for a hermitage. He planted some young bamboo nearby and spent his days in its vicinity. One day, when he was sweeping the path, a pebble flew and struck the bamboo, and when he heard the sound it made, he suddenly had a great satori. He bathed and purified himself and then went back to Tai-wi Mountain, where he burned incense and paid homage. Then he spoke to Ta-wei: "Ta-wei, Chief Priest, if you had answered me on that other occasion, how would this thing ever have been possible? The depths of your kindness exceed even those of my own parents." Then he composed this verse:

> With one blow of the pebble, everything I
>   knew perished.
> What more is there for me to practice, what
>   more to subdue?
> Moving about with ease, I conduct myself
>   in the ancient Way,
> And I never feel any despondency.
> Wherever I am, I leave no traces;
> It is conduct apart from forms and sounds.
> Those in all the directions who are
>   enlightened in the Way
> Are called "those of the highest talent."

He presented this to Ta-wei, who said, "How thorough you are."

Further, the Ch'an master Ling-yüan Chih-ch'in had practiced the Way for thirty years. Once, he was wandering around in the mountains, and as he paused at the foot of a hill, he saw a place where people lived. It was spring, and when he saw the blossoms on a peach tree, he immediately became enlightened. He composed a verse and presented it to Ta-wei. It said,

> For thirty years I have sought the
>   swordsman.
> How many times have the leaves fallen, or
>   the branches broken off?
> After once seeing the peach blossoms,
> There is nothing more to doubt.

Ta-wei said, "The person who enters the Way according to circumstances never again regresses." In other words, he acknowledged the enlightenment. Is there ever anyone who is not enlightened by circumstances? Does anyone ever slide back? I am not saying this only with regard to Chih-ch'in. Chih-ch'in finally became the Dharma heir of Ta-wei. If the forms of the mountains are not the pure body [of the Buddha], how could this happen?

105

A certain monk who was a disciple of Chang-sha Ching-ch'en asked him, "How can I unite the mountains, streams, and great earth within myself?" The master replied, "How can you unite yourself with the mountains, streams, and great earth?" What is meant here is that if you are not anything other than your true self, then whether you speak of yourself being united with the mountains, streams, and great earth, [or of the mountains, streams, and great earth being united with yourself], there should not be any obstacles between what unites and that with which one is united.

Huang-chao, who was the great master Hui-chüeh of Lang-yeh Mountain, was a distant descendant of Nan-yüeh's Dharma. Once, Tzu-hsüan, who gave lectures on the scriptures, asked him, "How does our pure, original nature instantly become mountains, streams, and the great earth?" Hui-chao tried to instruct him by asking him in turn, "How does our pure, original nature instantly give birth to the mountains, streams, and the great earth?" You must understand with regard to this that you should not mistakenly think that the original, pure nature as mountains, rivers, and the great earth, is the natural world of mountains, rivers, and the great earth. The person who just fumbles around in the sutras and has never heard this until now does not understand that the mountains, rivers, and the great earth are mountains, rivers, and the great earth. You must understand that if the pure nature, your original face, is not the forms of the mountains and the sound of the valley streams, then the expounding of the Dharma by holding up a flower did not occur, nor did the acquiring of the marrow [of Bodhidharma]. Because of the merits of the forms of the mountains and sounds of the streams, the world and all sentient beings in it become enlightened at the same time, and like the Buddha himself, see the morning star and become all the Buddhas.

These sentient beings I have been speaking of were superior people whose spirit in seeking the Dharma was extremely profound. We of the present time ought to use their acts as models for our own efforts. In the present time, also, true followers of the Way should arouse such a spirit without regard for fame and fortune. In this time and place, so far from the land of Śākyamuni, true seekers of the Way are rare indeed. They are not non-existent, but one does not encounter them often. Even though they take their home departure and seem to be divorced from worldly ways, they are just using the Way in order to acquire fame and fortune. It is shameful, deplorable, that they traffic in evil karma because they have ignored time. Sometime, they may abandon [their wickedness] and acquire the Way. For the time being, they do not love the true dragon, even though they may meet a true teacher. Śākyamuni referred to such fellows as pitiful examples of humanity. Such fellows have reached this end because of the evil karma of previous lives. Because they lack the spirit to seek the Dharma for the sake of the Dharma, when they do meet the true dragon and doubt whether they are seeing the real dragon, they are destroyed by it. Because their mind and body, bone and flesh, have never been born in accordance with the Dharma, they consequently are not fit for the Dharma, and they cannot accept it. This Way has been transmitted from master to disciple over and over in this manner down to the present time.

The mind which seeks satori is considered nowadays to be merely an ancient dream. How pitiful it is that, although you are born on the mountain of jewels, no one knows of these jewels or sees them. How will you ever acquire the Dharma treasure? If you arouse the thought of seeking enlightenment, then afterward, even if you are born among the six destinations or in one of the four manners of being born, the cause of your rebirth will be the practices and vows you made for the sake of satori. Thus, as it is said that just as the days and months of former times are all eternally past and gone, but one's present life is not yet over, so should one quickly make a vow. This vow is as follows: "I vow that I and all living beings in all lives from now on shall be able to hear the true Dharma, and when we hear it, we will be unable to doubt it, and it will be impossible not to have faith in it. When we come in contact with the true Dharma, we will abandon worldly ways and receive and accept the true Dharma. Later, the great earth and all sentient beings will achieve perfect Buddhahood."

If you make a vow in this way, it will be the proper condition for arousing the thought of enlightenment. Do not be negligent in this. Also, Japan is very far from foreign lands, and people here are extremely deluded. From ancient times until now, no saintly people have been born here, nor have there been any naturally intelligent people. Need I say that there have been no true followers of the Buddha's Way. When those who are ignorant of the mind which seeks the Way try to understand it, good advice hurts their ears, and while they resent others, they do not reflect upon themselves.

Now with regard to your practice and vows, whether or not you have aroused the thought of enlightenment, whether or not you are practicing, do not let others know about it. Practice in such a way that it is not known. Never speak of it yourself. People today do not truly seek the Way, so they do not practice with their bodies or enlighten their minds, but still they are praised by others and sought out as individuals in whom practice and enlightenment have been fulfilled. This is nothing but delusion within delusion, and this kind of confused thinking should cease.

The difficulty of hearing the Dharma and seeing the truth easily when one is seeking the Way is the labor of one's heart's desire in the search for the true teaching. This labor of one's heart's desire has been transmitted from patriarch to patriarch as the brilliant light of the Buddha and as the mind of the Buddha. From the days when the Tathagata dwelt in the world up to now there have always been those who were very concerned about fame and fortune in the practice of the Way. When they came in contact with the teaching of a true master and had a change of heart and began to really seek the

Dharma, they naturally acquired the Way.

Now, when you practice the Way, you should know that certain problems may arise. For instance, you may be one of those with a "beginner's mind" who arouses the first thought of enlightenment, or one of those whose practice is mature, or you may have the opportunity to give the teaching to others and transmit the Way, or you may not have the opportunity. You may be able to develop a fondness for the teaching of the ancient Buddha and learn it, or you may be deprived of it and simply become a demon who does not learn it. But whichever it may be, do not become attached to either or be distressed about either. However, people of today are really unconcerned about this, which is merely indifference to either attachment or distress. The reason they do not worry about it is that they do not know about the three root poisons [of desire, hatred, and ignorance]. You should never forget the determination you had at the time you first aroused a joyous feeling about the Buddha Way and began seeking it. That is, when you arouse the thought of enlightenment, you should seek the Dharma for the sake of others, and reject fame and fortune. Do not desire fame and fortune, but just desire to obtain the Way at once. Consequently, do not expect to have the respect of the nation's ruler and his retainers, and do not expect to be honored by them. Even though such a situation has occurred in the past in which a monk received respect and honor from the ruler and his retainers, that person did not want it and did not seek it. Thus, in seeking the Way, you should hope that you will not become restricted by the respect and honor of men and gods. However, the foolish people of the world, even though they have the mind which seeks the Way, lose their original determination quickly and mistakenly hanker after the honor of men and gods, pleased in their belief that they have gone as far as one can go in the Dharma. When the ruler and his retainers become eager to take refuge, these people think to themselves, "My Dharma has flowered to its fullest." This is one of the demons which appears when you undertake the Way. You should never neglect compassion for the ruler and his retainers, but you should not be delighted about it.

O monks, observe: the wise admonish us that even in the time of the Buddha there were, to quote the golden words of the Buddha, "many who slandered the Dharma even while following it." Thus, they damaged it. But stupid people do not understand the precious nature of the Buddha Way, so they harm it. These small, animal-like people are often considered to be among the assemblies of the wise, nevertheless. We also read that many of the Indian patriarchs were injured by nonbelievers, followers of the small vehicle, and rulers. It is not because the nonbelievers were superior people, or that those injured were lacking in the knowledge of all Buddhas. When Bodhidharma came to China from India and stayed at Shaolin Monastery, not even the Liang Emperor Wu knew about him, nor did the Emperor of Wei. At that time, however, there were two dogs, Bodhiruci and Hui-kuang, the vinaya master, who were experts in the scriptures. Their own reputations being false, they feared true followers of the Way, knowing that their own teachings would be obscured like the sun behind the clouds, and so they tried to slander the true teachings. These two were feared by true followers of the Way even more than Devadatta, who lived at the time of the Buddha. It is sad, but the fame and fortune they so ardently sought was hated by Bodhidharma even more than the defilement of excrement. This situation, however, is not the result of any deficiency in the Dharma, and there have always been dogs who howled at good men. Don't be disturbed by the howling dogs, and do not bear a grudge against them. Instead, vow to guide them, in accordance with the passage [in the *Brahmajala Sūtra*] which says, "Even though you are dogs, you should arouse the thought of enlightenment." Our predecessors said with regard to this, "They are just animals with human faces."[3] There are also among the human-faced animals some demons who take refuge in the Buddha and honor him. The Buddha said, "You should not associate with rulers, princes, retainers, high dignitaries, Brahmins, or laymen."[4] Truly, this method of practice should not be forgotten by any of you who wish to learn the Buddha's Way. In this manner, in the individual who is just beginning to seek the Way for the first time as a bodhisattva, merits will accumulate as he progresses.

Also, since ancient times, the great god Śakra has appeared on earth to test the spirit of the seeker of the Way, or else Māra has appeared to disturb his practices. This happens when the follower of the Way does not give up his yearning for fame and fortune. When great compassion and great wisdom are deep, and one makes the vow to deliver all beings to the other shore of enlightenment, then there are no obstacles in one's path. The power of one's own practice is enough to win the ruler to the Way, and you may also see this as one of the blessings of worldly life. At such a time, you must penetrate to the truth and not be blind. The ignorant will take great delight [in the conversion of the ruler], like foolish dogs gnawing on a dry bone. The wise will avoid this, just as ordinary people are revolted by excrement.

The person who has just aroused the thought of seeking the Way cannot fathom the Buddha Way by means of plotting and scheming. No matter how much he schemes, he never hits the mark. But even though he cannot enter the Way by plotting and scheming, this does not mean that he cannot attain the ultimate. The inner depths of attainment are not at all shallow in the same way that plotting and scheming are in the beginner. Therefore, you must just begin directly to train in the Way in the manner of those who have previously attained supreme *bodhi*. This means that you may have to climb the peaks of mountains and sail the deep oceans in order to visit a teacher and ask about the Way. If you call upon a teacher or solicit the help of a good friend, they descend from the heavens and appear out of the earth. As for the guidance of the true teacher, it is to be asked of sentient beings and even of insentient beings. Those who hear the teaching may hear it with their bodies or they may hear it with their minds. Hearing with one's ears is the usual way to do it, but hearing with one's eyes is also a way to penetrate to the truth. In seeing the Buddha, also, one may see one's own Buddha or the Buddha of others, one may see large Buddhas or small Buddhas. Don't be alarmed at seeing a large Buddha, and do not be troubled at seeing a small Buddha. Just recognize this so-called large Buddha or small Buddha as the forms of the mountains and the sounds of the valley streams. Here is the long, broad tongue of the Buddha, here are the myriad verses of the sutra which teach the Dharma. Here is the unobstructed, sovereign teaching of the Dharma, and here abides the one realm of satori. Worldly beings may say, "When we look about, everything is high, everything is broad." The Ch'an master Ju-ching said, "It is universally empty, it is universally overflowing." It is nothing more than the green of pines in the spring and the glory of chrysanthemums in autumn. When the good friend has reached the ground of satori, he becomes a great teacher of men and gods. While he has still not reached this ground but recklessly tries to show the Way, he is nothing more than a big robber who harms men and gods. What faith has he who does not know the true body which is the spring pine, or the true reality which is, just as it is, the autumn chrysanthemum? How can he ever cut off the roots of birth and death?

Moreover, the mind and body are lazy, and if you lack faith, you should show a sincere heart and make repentence before the Buddhas and patriarchs. If you do this, the power of the merit of repentence before the Buddhas will help and purify you. These merits create and sustain an unobstructible pure faith and diligence. Once this pure faith becomes evident, you yourselves and all others will be converted to the Buddha Way, and its benefits will extend everywhere to beings both sentient and insentient. This is what you should do to repent. Say, "I ask that even though my past bad karma has greatly accumulated in me and is a cause for the obstruction of the Way, all the Buddhas and patriarchs who have acquired the Way by means of the Buddha Way compassionately think of me and free me from my accumulated bad karma, and eliminate all the obstacles to my learning the Way. The merits of their Dharma teachings fill up the unbounded universe; may the Buddhas and patriarchs extend their compassion to me. In the past, the Buddhas and patriarchs were the same as we are now; in the future may we be the same as all Buddhas and patriarchs." When we see all the Buddhas, all alike are one Buddha, one patriarch; when we think of putting forth the thought of enlightenment, we and all Buddhas alike arouse the thought. With regard to extending compassion unlimitedly in all directions, sometimes we have the opportunity, and sometimes we do not. Thus, the Ch'an master Lung-ya said:

> Those in the past who were not
>   enlightened will now be enlightened;
> You ought to acquire this in this very life.
> When Buddhas were not enlightened, they
>   were like you are now;
> If you become enlightened now, you will
>   be like the old Buddhas.

You should reflect deeply on this verse by Lung-ya. Be responsible for your own enlightenment. If you repent in this way, you will surely receive help from all the Buddhas, help which cannot be detected with your eyes. Concentrate your mind, arrange your body properly, kneel, and make *gasshō*, and then repent all your past transgressions and evil acts before the Buddha. The power of repentence will destroy the roots of wickedness and make them vanish. This is the genuine, true practice, the mind which truly has faith, the body which truly has faith.

When you practice correctly, the sounds and forms of the valley streams and the forms and sounds of the mountains all become the myriad verses of the sutras. If you yourself do not prize fame and fortune or your own mind and body, and you are generous in abandoning them before the Buddhas and patriarchs, then the valley streams and mountains will be generous in preaching the Dharma. Now, as for whether the streams and mountains reveal the myriad verses or not, it is beyond the power of the discriminating mind to know, but they are still the myriad verses, without doubt. If yourself, who are the valley streams and mountains, cannot develop the power which illuminates the true reality of the mountains and valley streams, who else is going to be able to convince you that you and the streams and mountains are one and the same?

## NOTES

1. A reference to the well-known episode in which Hui-k'o cut off one of his arms and presented it to Bodhidharma in order to demonstrate his sincerity in seeking the Dharma. Dōgen mentions this episode several times in *Shōbōgenzō*, citing Hui-k'o as an example of the very strong determination required by one who seeks the Dharma. Hui-k'o eventually received the Dharma transmission from Bodhidharma, becoming the second Chinese Zen patriarch.

2. A well-known poet who lived during the Sung Dynasty in China.

3. The commentaries give the source of this quotation as the *Ta chih tu lun*, a lengthy commentary on the *Prajñāpāramitā Sūtra*.

4. From the *Lotus Sūtra*, in the chapter named "Easy Practice."

# HOTSU MUJŌ SHIN

*"Arousing the Supreme Thought"*

Śākyamuni Buddha says [in the *Nirvāna Sūtra*], "The Himalaya Mountains are just like great nirvana." This is a very pertinent figure of speech. It is a simile which accurately grasps the Himalayas just as they are. The point which Śākyamuni made in making a simile of the Himalayas is that they are like nirvana in their exalted height. The simile shows that both are identical in this respect.

However, Bodhidharma, the first Chinese patriarch, said, "The One Mind and all minds are wood and stone." What he calls "mind" is the absolute mind, the mind of the whole world, and so the One Mind is the mind of oneself and others. The minds of all the beings in the world, the minds of Buddhas and patriarchs everywhere, and the minds of *devas* and *nāgas* are wood and stone.[1] There is no mind apart from these. These stones and wood, or things in general, are not themselves bound by the realms of being and nonbeing, emptiness and form, and so on. One arouses the thought of enlightenment, practices, and attains with the mind which is wood and stone, because mind is wood and mind is stone. With the power of this mind which is wood and stone, the mind which is liberated now is manifested. Hearing and seeing the sounds and sights of the mind which is wood and stone, for the first time one transcends the views of those fellows outside the Dharma. There is no Buddha Dharma apart from this.

Nan-yang Ta-cheng said, "The rubble filling in the wall is the mind of the ancient Buddhas." You should understand this by carefully studying what and where the stone and wood rubble are which are mind as stone and wood. "The mind of the ancient Buddhas" should not be understood as something irrelevant to your experience, as some mind which exists from the beginningless past, for it is the mind which eats rice gruel or tastes other food in your ordinary, everyday life, it is the mind which is grass, the mind which is water. Within this kind of life just as it is is the act of sitting like a Buddha and making an effort like a Buddha which is called "arousing the thought of enlightenment."

The conditions for arousing the thought of enlightenment do not come from anywhere else. It is the enlightened mind which arouses the thought of enlightenment. The meaning of this phrase, "it is the enlightened mind which arouses the thought of enlightenment" is that one makes a stupa with a blade of grass, one makes a sutra scroll with a rootless tree, one honors the Buddha with a grain of sand, one honors the Buddha with the water in which rice has been soaked. One offers a handful of food to living creatures and one presents five flowers to the Tathagata; this is arousing the thought of enlightenment. Following the encouragement of others, practicing good to even the slight extent possible for you, bowing to the Buddha while you are being disturbed by demons, all these are also the arousing of the thought of enlightenment. Not only that, but knowing that one's home is not really one's home, abandoning home and going away from home, entering the mountains and practicing the Buddha's Way, practicing with faith [in the teacher] or practicing according to the Dharma [as found in the scriptures] is also arousing the thought of enlightenment. It is making the image of a Buddha, making a stupa, reading the sutras, being mindful of the Buddha, preaching the Dharma for living beings, visiting a true teacher and asking questions, and sitting cross-legged and doing zazen. It is also bowing to the Buddha, Dharma, and Sangha, and it is reciting, "I take refuge in the Buddha."

Such conditions as these myriad practices are all forms of arousing the thought of enlightenment. It is also acquiring the Way when putting forth the thought of enlightenment within a dream, or acquiring the Way when putting forth the thought while drunk.[2] Or else it is acquiring the Buddha Way by putting forth the thought when one sees the spring flowers scattered by the wind, or when one sees the autumn leaves falling.[3] Or else it is acquiring the Way by putting forth the thought while seeing peach blossoms, or hearing a pebble strike a green bamboo.[4] Or else it is acquiring the Way by putting forth the thought in the heavens or within the deep sea.[5] All these are examples of putting forth the thought of enlightenment within the thought of enlightenment. Putting forth the thought of enlightenment by means of the thought of enlightenment means putting forth the thought of enlightenment with one's own mind and body which are the Mind as rivers and mountains. It is putting forth the thought of enlightenment within the minds and bodies of all the Buddhas. It is putting forth the thought of enlightenment within the skin, flesh, bones, and marrow of all the Buddhas and patriarchs [which are your own skin, flesh, bone, and marrow].

This being so, the making of Buddha images and stupas at this time are surely the arousing of the thought of enlightenment. Directly achieving perfect Buddhahood is surely the arousing of the thought of enlightenment. But do not stop just halfway, [thinking that you can do such things as read sutras, think of the Buddha, make stupas, and so on, merely formally]. Such things must be unconditioned merits,[6] the merits of non-self-assertive action.[7] Arousing the thought of enlightenment means having a correct understanding in accordance with the truth, or having a correct understanding in accordance with the nature of the Dharma. It is samādhi which gathers together [the merits] of all the Buddhas. It is the realization of the *dhāranī's* of all the Buddhas. It is the mind of *anuttara samyak sambodhi*. It is the fruit of arhatship. It is the manifestation of the Buddha. Outside of this arousing of the thought of enlightenment, there is no Buddha Dharma such as the unconditioned and so on.

against Hinayana

In spite of this, the deluded followers of the small vehicle say, "Making Buddha images and erecting stupas are deeds done as mundane merit, so you should leave them alone and not do them. Stopping the discriminating mind and achieving one-pointedness of mind are unconditioned. The mind which neither arises nor ceases does nothing. This is reality. The close inspection of the true marks of the nature of dharmas is satori." Both in India and China, in ancient times and now, it has been a common custom to claim this sort of thing. Using this as a pretext, even though these people commit offenses against the precepts and are guilty of the five unpardonable acts, still they do not make Buddha images or erect stupas. Living in a world of passions as countless as the trees of a forest, dirtying themselves in muddy water as they do, they do not think of the Buddha nor do they read the sutras. They not only damage the Buddha seed of those who live in this world, but they even deny the very Buddha nature of the Tathāgata.

Truly this is regrettable. Even though they have been fortunate enough to meet the Buddha, Dharma, and Sangha, they still have become the bitter enemies of the Three Jewels. While they climb the mountain of the Three Jewels, they return with empty hands, and though they enter the ocean of the Three Jewels, they return with empty hands. Because of the existence of this state of affairs, even though a million Buddhas and patriarchs are revealed in the world, these fellows never find the opportunity to come into contact with the Buddha Way, and they lose their grasp on the bodhi mind. The reason is that they do not follow the sutras, nor do they follow the advice of a good friend who wishes to help them. Rather, they follow false teachers who are outside the Way. The false view that making Buddha images and erecting stupas is not the same as arousing the thought of enlightenment should be abandoned at once. Do not pay any attention to false teachings and views about washing the mind, washing the body, washing the ears, or washing the eyes. At once be in accord with the Buddha's scriptures, follow a true teacher, take refuge in the true Buddha Dharma, and learn and practice the Buddha Dharma.

In the great Way of the Buddha Dharma, all the sutra chapters in the universe are contained within a dust mote. Within a dust mote, an incalculable number of Buddhas dwell. A blade of grass or a leaf are the Mind and Body. If the myriad forms do not rise, neither does the One Mind rise. If all things are the revelation of ultimate reality,[8] then a single dust mote is the revelation of ultimate reality. Therefore, the One Mind is all things, all things are the One Mind, they are the total Body. If such things as making stupas is a conditioned effort, then bodhi, that is to say Buddha result, and Buddha nature themselves must be conditioned also. However, because Buddha nature is not conditioned, neither is making Buddha images or erecting a stupa a conditioned act. They are the non-self-assertive acts of arousing the thought of enlightenment, and their merits are unconditioned and pure. Truly, they must be experienced, believed, and understood as the arousing of the thought of enlightenment. The eternal practice of the Way and the vow to emancipate all living beings are based on this arousing of the thought of enlightenment and are born from it. This arousing of the thought of enlightenment does not decay ever. It is called seeing the

Buddha and hearing the Dharma.

You should understand that gathering together wood and stone, piling up mud and clay, and collecting gold, silver, and the seven precious stones and making a Buddha image or stupa is the same as making images and stupas by collecting together the One Mind. It is gathering together emptiness upon emptiness and making a Buddha. It is using mind upon mind and creating a Buddha. It is piling stupa upon stupa to make a stupa. It is manifesting Buddha upon Buddha and making a Buddha. Consequently, the "Skillful Means" chapter of the *Lotus Sutra* says, "When you have this thought, all the Buddhas in the universe are revealed." You should understand that thinking just once of becoming a Buddha is the revelation of all the Buddhas in the universe. When one thing becomes a Buddha, all things become Buddhas. When Śākyamuni attained enlightenment, he said, "When the morning star appeared, I and the great earth with all its beings simultaneously became Buddhas." Therefore, arousing the thought of enlightenment, practice, bodhi and nirvana are all simultaneous with the enlightenment, practice, bodhi and nirvana of Śākyamuni. What we call the body and mind in the Buddha Way is grass, trees and wall rubble; it is wind, rain, water and fire. When you reflect on these things and cause the development of the Buddha Way, it is arousing the thought of enlightenment. Using space to make an image of the Buddha or to erect a stupa is arousing the thought of enlightenment. Scooping up the valley streams is making a Buddha image or stupa. It is the arousal of *anuttara samyak sambodhi.* It is a myriad arousings of one thought of enlightenment. The same is true with regard to practice and attainment.

However, if your understanding is that arousing the thought of enlightenment is just a single arousing of the thought of enlightenment and that there are no other arousings, and that while practices are numerous, attainment is a single attainment, you do not really understand the Buddha

Dharma nor can you grasp it, nor can you come into contact with it. A myriad arousings of the thought of enlightenment are surely one arousing; the arousing of the thought of enlightenment by a myriad people is the arousing of the thought by a single person. The arousing of the thought of enlightenment by a single person is the arousing of the thought by a myriad people. The same is true of practice, attainment, and the turning of the wheel of the Dharma. If your own body and mind are not grass, wood, and so on, then they are not your body and mind. And if your own body and mind do not exist, neither do grass and wood. If grass and wood do not exist, then they are not grass and wood.

The practice of zazen and learning the Way are the arousal of the thought of enlightenment. Arousing the thought of enlightenment is neither identical with zazen nor different from it, and zazen is neither the same as the arousal of the thought of enlightenment nor different from it, nor are they two things, nor are they three, nor are they different. You should study everything in the same way.

From beginning to end, when you collect grass and wood and the seven precious stones and use them to make a Buddha image or stupa, if you feel that you cannot achieve the Buddha Way because these are conditioned acts, then the thirty-seven parts of enlightenment are also conditioned. Practicing the Way with the mind and body of a human being or god is also conditioned. If this is the case, you will not achieve the ultimate stage.

Grass, wood, wall rubble, the four elements, and the five *skandhas* are all identical in being nothing but Mind;[9] they are all alike true mark.[8] All the worlds in the ten directions are ultimate reality, Buddha nature, all are identically Dharma abode, Dharma state.[10] Within ultimate reality and Buddha nature there are no grass, wood, or wall rubble; within grass, wood, and wall rubble, there is no ultimate reality or Buddha nature. Dharmas are not mundane and conditioned, nor are they supramundane and unconditioned; they are the manifestation of ultimate reality, they are just what they are in themselves. "Things being just what they are in themselves" are "thus," absolute reality. This "thus" is your present body and mind. It is within this body and mind that you should arouse the thought of enlightenment. Do not dislike treading on water or stone.[11] Just use a blade of grass to make a six-foot golden Buddha body, or use a speck of dust to build a stupa to the ancient Buddhas, and this itself is arousing the thought of enlightenment. It is seeing the Buddha and it is hearing the Buddha. It is seeing the Dharma and hearing the Dharma. It is becoming a Buddha and acting like a Buddha.

Śākyamuni Buddha said, "The upasaka and the upasika and the sons and daughters of good family honor the Three Jewels with the flesh of their wives and children, and they honor the Three Jewels with their own flesh. After monks have received these alms of faith, they surely must practice." This being so, what you must understand is that honoring the Three Jewels with food, clothing, bedding, medicine, monasteries, fields and woodlands is to do honor with one's own body, and the flesh, skin, bone and marrow of one's wife and children. When these merge with the ocean of merits of the Three Jewels, all become one. When they become one, they are the Three Jewels. The merits of the Three Jewels becoming a reality in your own body and in the skin, flesh, bones and marrow of your wife and children is the earnest and vigorous effort of learning the Way. Considering the World-honored One's nature and teachings to be your own nature and teachings means considering the skin of the Buddha Way to be your own skin; it means considering the flesh of the Buddha Way to be your own flesh; it means considering the bones of the Buddha Way to be your own bones; it means considering the marrow of the Buddha Way to be your own marrow. What is called "alms of faith" is the arousing of the thought of enlightenment, and the monk who receives it should practice. The giver must be a true giver, and the recipient must be a true recipient.

When the thought of enlightenment, which may be no bigger than a speck of dust, is aroused, the One Mind is aroused with it. When the One Mind is aroused for the first time, the one emptiness is also aroused in an instant. When all Buddhas and ordinary beings have aroused the thought of enlightenment, then for the first time the one Buddha nature which has existed all along in seed form is realized. When you use the total power of the four elements and five skandhas and practice earnestly, you will acquire the Way. This is because the four elements and five skandhas, grass, wood, and wall rubble are all identically involved in practice, and because all are identical in their nature [i.e., all are Buddha nature]. They have the same mind, the same life, the same body, and the same activity.

There have been many disciples of the Buddha patriarchs who learned the Way by making the mind of grass and wood their own mind. This is the sign of the arousing of the thought of enlightenment. The fifth patriarch was once employed as a tree planter. Lin-chi made his practice the planting of cedar and pine when he was at Mount Huang-po. There is the story of an old man by the name of Lo, who was a contemporary of Tung-shan Wu-pen, who also planted pines. All gouged out the eyes of the Buddha patriarchs [and made them their own] using the high moral principles of pine and oak. This is fervently practicing the Way by practically utilizing the ability to make the eyes of the Buddhas and patriarchs your own. Making Buddha images and stupas and so on are all ways of using their eyes. It is tasting the arousing of the thought of enlightenment. It is using the arousing of the thought of enlightenment. Therefore, those who cannot acquire the eyes of stupa building and Buddha making cannot achieve the Way of the Buddhas and patriarchs. As soon as you acquire the eyes which consist of making a Buddha image, you become a Buddha, you become a patriarch.

Some say, "The Buddha images and stupas later turn back to earth again, and so the merit of making them cannot be real, but training is like durable metal which does not turn back to earth," but this is not the teaching of the Buddha. If it is claimed that the stupa which has been erected is changed back to earth again, the unproduced also returns to earth again. If the unproduced does not return to earth again, neither does the stupa become earth again. According to the Buddhas and patriarchs, "Within these [activities] is the abiding place of 'this.' It is called nirvana and samsara."

According to a sutra, "When a bodhisattva confronting samsara first arouses the thought of enlightenment and earnestly seeks bodhi, he becomes firm and unshakeable. The merits of this one thought are deep, extensive, boundless. If the Tathagata were to discuss and distinguish them for many eons, he could not exhaust their number." You should clearly understand that using samsara to arouse the thought of enlightenment is the same as earnestly seeking bodhi. His one thought is identical with [the life of] a single blade of grass or a tree, because it is one life and one death.

However, the depths of these merits are limitless, and they are boundless in breadth. Their number cannot be exhausted even though the Tathagata discusses and distinguishes them for many eons. Even though the ocean may be dried up, its bottom remains, and even though a man die, his mind [i.e., his will, or karma] remains, so it cannot be exhausted either. And just as this one thought is deep, broad, and boundless, so is a blade of grass, a tree, a stone, or a tile also boundless in depth and breadth. If the grass or stone is seven or eight feet high, then so is this one thought seven or eight feet high.

This being so, entering the deep mountains and thinking about the Buddha Way is comparatively easy, while building stupas and making Buddha images [which are the arousing of the thought of enlightenment] is very difficult. Although both are achieved through energy and the lack of neglect and laziness, using mind [as one's own] and having one's mind and body used by mind are very different. Arousing the thought of enlightenment in such a way goes on manifesting Buddha patriarchs eternally.

## NOTES

1. This means that Buddha, living beings, and insentient things are all the One Mind.

2. Allusions to two episodes in the *Lotus Sutra* and *Ta chih tu lun* respectively. The story of the drunken Brahmin who received the precepts and made his home departure while drunk is told in Dōgen's *Shukke* ("Home Departure"). There, he cites the 13th volume of the *Ta chih tu lun* as his source.

3. From the *Mahāvibhāsā, Taishō* no. 1545.

4. Allusions to two well-known enlightenment experiences. When Ling-yüan was wandering in the mountains, he unexpectedly came upon a place where some people were living, and when he saw the peach blossoms, he became enlightened. The second case is that of Hsiang-yen Chih-hsien, who was sweeping the path of his hermitage and became enlightened when he heard the sound of a pebble striking a bamboo. Both incidents are discussed in Dōgen's *Keisei sanshoku* ("The sounds of the valley streams and the forms of the mountains").

5. Both incidents are derived from the *Lotus Sūtra*.

6. 無作. Either "unconditioned," or "unmade," which really mean the same, both being translations of the Sanskrit *asamskrita*.

7. 無為. This also means "unconditioned," but to avoid repetition of the term used above, I have adopted the Taoist meaning of "non-self-assertive." It refers to an act which is not performed for self-gratification.

8. 実相. Sometimes translated as "real-mark," or "true-mark" (Richard Robinson and others), and sometimes, as here, "the revelation of ultimate reality." It is the mark which all things possess, consisting of being just what they are in themselves. A synonym would be "suchness" or "isness," sometimes used as a translation of the Sanskrit *tathatā*.

9. 唯心

10. Dharma-state *(hō-i)*: this refers to the specific temporal and spacial location of what we may term as "event;" i.e., something concrete taking place. This event is *just that* and nothing else, containing within itself the totality of a specific experience, with no limiting or partial elements. "Thus the act of eating, for example, is viewed as the absolute given, self-sufficient in itself; it is the *kōan* realized in life *(genjōkōan)"* (Hee-jin Kim, *Dōgen Kigen: Mystical Realist*, U. of Arizona Press, 1975, p. 200.

11. References to stories about the Zen masters Tung-shan and Hui-neng. The reference to Hui-neng concerns his treading in the stone mortar while pounding rice, even though he had already acquired the Dharma.

# SHUKKE

*"Home Departure"*

The *Ch'an yüan ch'ing kuei*[1] says, "All the Buddhas of the past, future, and present have taught <u>home departure</u> and achievement of the Way. All the twenty-eight Indian patriarchs and the six Chinese patriarchs who have transmitted the seal of the Buddha mind were *śramaṇas*. All who left the home life were afterwards able to become the teachers of the three worlds because they upheld the moral precepts *(śīla)* of the Buddha Way. Consequently, when you practice Zen and seek the true teacher, you should give priority to the observance of these precepts. If you do not free yourselves from worldly delusion and dissociate yourselves from evil acts by upholding the pure precepts of the Buddha Way, there is no way for you to ever become a Buddha or patriarchal teacher. You must receive the precepts *(jukai).*"

"In order to receive the precepts of home departure, you must supply yourselves with the three robes, bowl, eating utensils, cushion, and new underclothes. If you do not have new underclothes, you may use some that have been washed, but when you enter the place where you are going to receive the precepts, you must not use someone else's robes and bowl. Concentrate single-mindedly on the Buddha Way, be modest in mind and body, model yourself on the Buddha, unite the precepts to your own mind and body, and make the Buddha mind your own mind. This is very important in the life of home departure, so do not neglect it. If you just borrow robes and bowl and go where the precepts are given, it will be as if you had not received them. If you do not receive the precepts by following these regulations, you are probably the kind of person who will not be able to receive the precepts in this life. By entering the Dharma gate carelessly, you become the kind of person who received the offering of the faithful in vain. When you are introduced to the Way for the first time and still do not understand the precepts, then if your teacher does not teach them to you, he is leading you down the wrong path. Therefore, I am now giving you this frank advice. I hope very much that you will engrave it on your hearts and never forget it. If you receive the precepts of the *śrāvakas* of the small vehicle, you should next be diligent about receiving the bodhisattva precepts, because this is the proper sequence of entering the door of the Dharma."

Clearly understand that the achievement of the Way by all the Buddhas and patriarchs was only through home departure and receiving the precepts. The life pulse of the Buddhas and patriarchs is only home departure and receiving the precepts. If you still have not made your home departure, neither are you a Buddha patriarch. Seeing the Buddha, seeing the patriarchs, is making your home departure and receiving the precepts.

Mahākāśyapa[2] left the home life to follow the Buddha in his wish to be freed of all defilements. The Buddha said to him, "Welcome, monk," and his hair and beard spontaneously fell to the ground and his body was spontaneously covered with monks' robes. It is clear from the traces we have of all the Buddhas that all who practiced the Way and freed themselves from defilements have made their home departure and received the precepts.

According to the third volume of the *Large Sutra on the Perfection of Wisdom*,[3] the Buddha, the World-Honored One, said, "If a bodhisattva, a great being, thinks, 'Someday I will surely abandon the ranks of the court and leave the home life, and on that day I will attain supreme bodhi. Also, on that day, when I leave the home life, I will turn the wonderful wheel of the Dharma and cause countless, numberless beings to abandon wickedness and delusion and produce the pure Dharma vision. Then I will cause them to exterminate their impurities forever and become wise and emancipated. Moreover, I will cause them to become irreversible in supreme bodhi,' then this bodhisattva who desires to accomplish such a thing should extensively study the *[Sutra on the] Perfection of Wisdom*."

Supreme enlightenment is acquired on the day one leaves the home life and receives the precepts. If there is no day of home departure, there is no day of supreme enlightenment. Thus, the dawning of the day of your home departure is the dawning of the day when you achieve supreme bodhi, and the dawning of the day when you achieve supreme bodhi is the dawning of the day of your home departure. This is the day when your layman's body, just as it is, is transformed into a Buddha's body, and you attain supreme bodhi and preach the Dharma for the sake of all beings. Your home departure itself causes many living beings to enter the Buddha Way. It is the practice of self-benefit and benefit to others which causes them to experience supreme bodhi and acquire irreversibility.

You should understand that when you have perfected this self-benefit and benefit to others, this is itself the seeking of supreme bodhi and becoming irreversible, and this immovability is nothing other than leaving the home life and receiving the precepts. Attaining supreme bodhi enlightens us to the fact that the day of home departure is the day of supreme bodhi. What you should understand correctly is that the day of home departure is the day when the opposition between bodhi and the first thought of enlightenment is transcended. This absolute time is the time of liberation. The day of home departure is the day when you know from inner experience that the time of three incalculable eons is the eternal now of the day of home departure. This day of home departure contains within itself the time when you dwell in the boundless oceans of the eons and teach the Dharma to all beings. The time of home departure is not a small period of time, such as that required for eating a meal, nor is it the unthinkable time of sixty small eons; it is time which transcends time. It is time which freed the Buddha's topknot. The day of home departure even transcends the day of home departure. The day of home departure is truly the day of home departure when you have overcome attachment and reached the state of dropping off mind and body. The day of achieving the Way is the day of achieving the Way; that is, the day of home departure is the day when you achieve the Way, and the day when you achieve the Way is the day of home departure.

The following is recorded in the thirteenth volume of the *Ta chih tu lun*:[4] "When the Blessed One was staying in the Jetavana Grove, a drunken Brahmin came to the Buddha and said that he wanted to leave the home life. At this, the Buddha had some monks shave off his hair and dress him in the robes of a monk. The Brahmin sobered up and was surprised to discover his altered appearance, and he left. Some monks then asked the Buddha why he had allowed the Brahmin to leave the home life. The Buddha replied, 'Never in all the ages up to now has that Brahmin ever thought of home departure. Now while he was drunk, it was a small matter for him to think that he wanted to leave the home life, but because this happened, in a later time he will really leave the home life.' " Thus, there are various conditions for home departure.

It is better to break the precepts as one who has left the home life than to observe them as a householder, because a householder cannot be liberated by the precepts.

You should understand the truth of the Buddha's words. The fundamental requirement of the Way is home departure. He who has not yet left the home life cannot acquire the Buddha Dharma. When the Buddha was still in the world, various non-believers had already given up their wicked ways through their own faith, but when they took refuge in the Buddha Dharma, they necessarily asked for home departure and the precepts.

Sometimes the Blessed One himself says in a friendly manner, "Welcome, monk," and thereby acknowledges home departure, and sometimes he gathers monks about him and has them shave their hair and beards and thus leave the home life and receive the precepts. In both cases, the Dharma of home departure and receiving the precepts is fulfilled in the minds and bodies of these people. You should understand how great are the merits of home departure and receiving the precepts. When the Buddha's efforts flood the minds and bodies of these people, their hair falls spontaneously to the ground and the kesa covers their bodies. If the Buddha does not acknowledge home departure, their hair is not shaved and the kesa does not cover the body. This means that the person has not yet received the Buddha's precepts. This being so, home departure and receiving the precepts is the new prediction of all Buddha Tathagatas that Buddhahood is certain.

Śākyamuni Buddha said, "Sons of good family, the Tathagata perceives that those who practice the Dharma in the small vehicle are slight of merit and laden with impurities, and it is for their sake that I left the home life and attained supreme bodhi when I was young. However, in truth, my experience of bodhi really occurred many, many ages ago. Now, in the present time, I exercise skillful means in order to educate beings and cause them to enter the Dharma, and so I say this. Although I experienced bodhi long, long ago, I say that I left the home life when young. 'I attained supreme bodhi' means 'I made my home departure when young.' When I departed the home life when young, beings who followed the small vehicle and whose merits were few and whose impurities were many left the home life with me when I was young. When I experienced the Dharma teaching of 'home departure when I was young,' I experienced the Buddha's enlightenment. So, in order to aid beings who delight in the Dharma of the small vehicle, I say that I left the home life when young and experienced supreme enlightenment." This may be so, but it still may be asked what the merits of home departure are. The answer is that the merits of home departure are countless and unlimited.

## NOTES

1. The *Ch'an yüan ch'ing kuei* is a well known list of monastic regulations of Chinese origin *(ch'ing kuei* are monastic regulations, which the Japanese call *shingi),* and is one of several such documents. *Ch'ing kuei* give detailed instructions for the living of the monastic life, including eating, bathing, interrelations between superiors and inferiors, use of the toilets and libraries, and so on. This *ch'ing kuei* was brought to Japan by Dōgen. It is said to be related in spirit to the *Pai-chang ch'ing kuei,* the first of its kind in Chinese Zen.

2. Mahākāśyapa was the spiritual successor of Śākyamuni, according to the Zen lineage charts.

3. *The Large Sutra on the Perfection of Wisdom* is the *Pañcaviṃśati-sāhasrikā prajñāpāramitā sūtra,*the best known of the longer versions of this literature.

4. A lengthy commentary on the above sutra, ascribed to Nāgārjuna but suspected to have been composed by its supposed translator into Chinese, Kumārajīva.

# RAIHAI TOKUZUI

*"Paying Homage and Acquiring the Essence"*

When one is involved in the cultivation of *anuttara samyak sambodhi,* it is most difficult to find the proper master. This master has nothing at all to do with such characteristics as male and female and so on, but the teacher must be one who is intimately acquainted with satori, one who is of the highest rank. The teacher is neither a young person nor an old person, and even if the teacher is the apparition of a wild fox, he will be a good teacher. The teacher has the appearance of one who has acquired the marrow of the Dharma,[1] and he will guide and benefit beings. He is one who does not disregard the law of cause and effect. He may be "you," "me," or "him" for the true teacher is completely empty.

As soon as a person meets a true teacher, he should cast off all the myriad conditions and, without wasting a second, vigorously study the Way. He should do zazen and learn the Way whether with no thought, with thought, or with half-thoughts. But in any case, he should practice single-mindedly, like one trying to extinguish a blaze in his hair, or like one standing on one foot. Acting in this way, he will not be troubled by demons who slander the Dharma. He is none other than the second patriarch, who cut off his own arm in order to acquire the essence. He himself is none other than the teacher who has cast off mind and body.

Acquiring the essence of the Dharma and transmitting it necessarily depends on sincerity and faith. Sincerity and faith are not things which come from outside or inside; they are only acquired by valuing the Dharma and transforming oneself completely. They are acquired by renouncing the world and making the Way one's real home. If one thinks even a little of his own body, and values it more than the Dharma, he will not acquire the Way nor will he transmit it. The spirit which values the Way is not one or two, but even though we do not expect to get the teaching of another, let us provisionally accept it as one or two. That is to say, if the mind treasures the Dharma, then one's helper may be a pillar, a lantern, all the Buddhas, a fox, a demon, male or female, but if one protects and supports the great Dharma in his own body, if he has received the essence of all the Buddhas and patriarchs, and if he has cast off mind and body, then even for countless eons he will devote his own mind and body to the practice of the Way. Acquiring a mind and body is fairly easy, just as rice, hemp, bamboo and reeds exist in the world in great numbers, but it is rare to meet the Dharma.

Śākyamuni Buddha said, "When you meet a teacher who expounds the matter of supreme bodhi, you should not think about his family lineage, pay attention to his appearance, pay any heed to his shortcomings, or criticize his actions. But because you value the wisdom of prajna, you should feed him daily to the extent of a million *ryō* in gold. Pay homage to him with food fit for celestial beings. Three times daily you should pay homage and honor him, and never make him troubled in his mind. In this manner the Way of bodhi will surely appear. Since I first put forth the thought of enlightenment up to now, I have practiced in this way, and I have acquired the highest enlightenment."

Therefore, you should entreat trees and rocks to preach the Dharma, and you should ask rice fields and gardens for the truth. Ask pillars for the Dharma, and learn from hedges and walls. Long ago the great god Indra honored a wild fox as his own master and sought the Dharma from him, calling him "Great Bodhisattva." It had nothing to do with whether the teacher was in a high or low form because of past karma.

However, deluded beings who have not heard the Buddha's Dharma think, "I am a high monk with much seniority and I cannot honor young monks even if they have acquired the Dharma. I have been engaged in practice for many years, and I cannot honor someone who has become a monk late in life, even if he has acquired the Dharma. I have been given the title of master, and I cannot honor someone who is not a master, even if he has acquired the Dharma. I am an important administrator in the clergy, and I cannot honor an ordinary monk, even if he has acquired the Dharma. I am a high priest, and I cannot honor laymen and laywomen, even if they have acquired the Dharma. I have reached a very high stage of the bodhisattva path, and I cannot honor nuns and others, even if they have acquired the Dharma. I am related by blood to the ruling family, and I cannot honor those who are not, even if they have acquired the Dharma." These foolish people abandon their fatherland and vainly tread the byways of foreign lands, and consequently they cannot see the Buddha's path.

Long ago during the T'ang Dynasty there was a great master named Chao-chou (Jōshū) who had aroused the thought of enlightenment, and when he set out on a pilgrimage he made this vow: "Even if the person is only seven years old, if he is my superior, I shall seek the teaching from him. Even if he is a hundred years old, if he is inferior to me, I shall teach him." If a person seeks the Dharma from a seven year old, the older person should pay homage to him. Truly, this is the spirit of the great man. He is one who has the spirit of the ancient Buddhas. If a nun appears who has acquired the Way, who has acquired the Dharma, the monk who is seeking the Dharma should become her disciple, and asking her about the Dharma and paying homage to her is the mark of a person who excels in practicing the Buddha Way. It is like looking for drinking water when you are thirsty.

Zen master Chih-hsien was a great master who was a disciple of Lin-chi. When Lin-chi saw him coming to his place for the first time, he welcomed him to stay there, at which Chih-hsien assented. Lin-chi said to him, "Stay with me for awhile as my disciple." Thus, Chih-hsien became his disciple. Later, he left Lin-chi and went to see a nun named Mo-shan. Mo-shan asked, "Where did you come from?" "I come from Lu-k'ou." (Literally, "I come from mouth-of-the road village.") Mo-shan replied, "Then why didn't you close it when you came here?" To this, Chih-hsien had no answer. He honored her with a bow and thus became her disciple. Later, he asked Mo-shan, "What is a summit mountain?" (i.e., *Mo-shan* means "summit (or peak) mountain.") Mo-shan said, "It is the mountain summit which cannot be seen by a person because it is shrouded in clouds." Chih-hsien then asked, "Who is this person in the mountains?" Mo-shan said, "It has no male or female form; it transcends form." Again Chih-hsien posed a question, "[If it is neither male nor female, then if it is just the apparition of a fox,] why not change it into some other form?" Said Mo-shan, "Since it is not a fox apparition, I will not transform it into anything." Chih-hsien just bowed. Consequently, he aroused the thought of enlightenment, and stayed there to be supervisor of the fields for three years. Later, as chief priest of a monastery, he said to a group of monks, "When I was with the compassionate father Lin-chi, I got half a dipper full; at the compassionate mother Mo-shan's, I got the other half. Both halves united into the full Buddha Dharma, and still today I am completely filled with the Dharma water of satori."

Now, reflecting on this story, Mo-shan was a prominent disciple of Kao-an Ta-yü. Her power of satori was superior, and she became the mother who taught Chih-hsien. Lin-chi had inherited the Dharma of the great Zen master Huang-po. His was the great power of practice, and he became the father of Chih-hsien. The father was male and the mother was female. Chih-hsien showed that he had a superior spirit when he sought the Dharma from Mo-shan and paid homage to her. He was unflagging in his pursuit of later training, and he is famous for seeking the Dharma without consideration of male and female.

Miao-hsin was a nun and the disciple of Hui-chi. One time, Hui-chi was about to select a monk to be chief in charge of external affairs, and he sought out some older monks, asking them, "I wonder who is most fit to become chief of external affairs?" After getting several suggestions, he said, "Even though Hsien-huai tzu (i.e., Miao-hsin) is a woman, she has the spirit of the superior person, and she is the most suitable for the position." All the monks there assented to this. Thus, Miao-hsin came to be chief in charge of external affairs. At that time, the advanced disciples of Hui-chi did not find this to be unsatisfactory. Even though this was not a very important position, we cannot overlook the fact that she was selected.

Later, when Miao-hsin was occupied as chief of external affairs, a party of seventeen monks from Szechwan who were visiting the great teachers of various areas came to Yang-shan to pay their respects, and they stayed in the guest house. While resting that night, they had a conversation concerning the famous *mondo* about the wind and the flag.[2] None of what the seventeen monks said really hit the mark. Miao-hsin, on the other side of the wall, heard what they said and made this comment: "Seventeen blind donkeys walk the road and without a bit of regret use up any number of straw sandals. But the Buddha Dharma is never found in a dream." Some lay people who were with Miao-hsin heard her criticism and related it to the seventeen monks. None of them felt any resentment about being criticized by the chief of external affairs. They realized that they still had not acquired the Way, and at once they made their robes neat, lit incense and paid homage, and renewed their vows. Miao-hsin sent a request for them to appear before her. When they were gathered before her, she said to them, "It is not the wind which moves, it is not the flag which moves, and it is not the mind which moves." Having heard this, the seventeen monks were enlightened. They made bows and became her disciples. Then they directly returned west to Szechwan and no longer stayed on Yang-shan. Truly, such an example as this cannot be found among those in the higher stages of bodhisattva practice;[3] it was the act of those who have transmitted the Dharma directly from all the Buddhas and patriarchs.

Therefore, when the chief priest of the monastery and his deputy are not around, you should look for a nun who has acquired the Way. Even if a monk is older and has been ordained for a long time, if he has not acquired the Dharma, do not try to use him. The person who is responsible for guiding those who are involved in practice must certainly be a person who has opened his Dharma eye.

However, ignorant people who are rigidly chained to external appearances and become objects of ridicule even from a worldly standpoint are indeed numerous. How much truer it is in the Dharma. There is no doubt that there are many who will not pay homage to women or nuns, even if they have acquired the Dharma and transmitted it. They do not understand the Dharma, and since they do not study the Dharma, they are like animals, far removed from the Buddhas and patriarchs.

If you just earnestly abandon your own mind and body to the Buddha Dharma with a firm resolution, the Buddha Dharma will surely reveal itself to you. Even among foolish humans and gods, hearts are moved by the truth, for how can the true Dharma of all the Buddhas not compassionately move the sincere heart? In earth, stones, sand, and pebbles, there is to be found the extremely inconceivable Mind which moves the sincere heart.

In the monasteries and temples of contemporary Sung China, there are places where nuns practice the Dharma, and if it is heard that a nun has acquired the Buddha Dharma, the emperor issues an imperial edict making her the chief priest of a monastery. This means that she preaches the Dharma in the Dharma Hall of the monastery. The nuns who study under her congregate in the Dharma Hall, and while standing, conduct the ceremonies of the Dharma Hall and hear the Dharma preached. There is also an exchange of questions and answers *(mondo)*. This has been the custom since ancient times. In other words, one who has acquired the Dharma is a real ancient Buddha, and no other so-called Buddha from earlier times is likely to be encountered. When the person in training meets me (and I have acquired the Dharma), he interviews me on the entirely new level of Buddha patriarch. When I, who have acquired the Dharma, meet him who is a trainee, yesterday is forgotten, and I interview him in the present which is only the present. For instance, when you make Dharma inquiries of a nun who transmits the treasury of the eye of the true dharma, who has reached the stage of arhat and pratyekabuddha, who has reached the stages of the bodhisattva's last ten stages, and you pay homage to her, the nun will naturally receive your homage. What is there intrinsically about a male to esteem? The body is empty, like the sky, empty is empty, the four elements are the four elements, and the five aggregates are the five aggregates wherever they are found. The female is no different from a male, so both male and female acquire the Dharma without distinction. It is nothing more than taking seriously the experience of the Buddha Way, so do not think about such differences as male and female. This is the most basic law of the Buddha Way.

Also, in Sung China, a practicing householder is a person who has not yet made his home departure and become a monk or nun. He lives in a hermitage, and his wife lives with him. Sometimes there are people who live celibate lives, and they are said to still be afflicted with delusion and turmoil. However, be that as it may, if they are truly involved in practice, honor their teacher, and search for the Dharma, they are no different from someone who has made his home departure. Even though one is a woman, even though one is an animal, it is the same.

He who still does not see the truth of the Buddha Way, even if he is an aged monk a hundred years old, is not the equal of a man or woman who has acquired the Way. These old monks are not to be given the three bows of homage, although they are entitled to the courtesy due to a host or superior. But they are not to be given any special homage.

Even a seven-year-old girl who practices the Buddha Dharma and is enlightened in it is the leader and guide of the fourfold community of Buddhists, the compassionate parent of living beings.[4] For instance, the *nāga* maiden in the *Lotus Sutra* achieved Buddhahood. Giving respect and homage to someone such as her is the same as giving it to all the Buddhas. That is, it is the ancient etiquette of the Buddha Way. If you cannot understand this, you will regrettably be unable to transmit the Buddha Way.

There have been women who have ascended the throne in China and Japan both in ancient times and recently. These lands are possessions of the throne, so the inhabitants of these countries are the subjects of the ruler. The people respect the ruler not as a person but for the rank. It is the same with regard to nuns; from ancient times they have been respected not as people but because they have experienced the Buddha Way.

Nuns who reach the stage of arhat[5] acquire the merits of the four fruits[6] and they conform [mentally and physically] to these merits. There are few among humans or celestial beings whose merits exceed those of the four fruits. All fall short of these merits. Since these merits are lacking in humans and celestials, such beings respect them. Who would not respect someone who has aroused the Buddha mind of the bodhisattva and transmits the true Dharma? Anyone who does not, slights himself, for he is himself the supreme enlightenment, and if he does not respect it, he is a fool who slanders the Dharma.

In Japan, the daughters of rulers and courtiers are like imperial consorts, and being like consorts, they have sometimes received royal titles. Some of these women have become nuns, while others have not. However, when monks who hanker for fame and fortune approach this kind of woman, they prostrate themselves at her feet and pay reverence to her. They are worse than servants of the ruler. How many of them will grow old as manservants of these women! It is sad that because they were born in a small country on the periphery of things they do not understand that this behavior is wrong. This does not happen in India or China but only in our own country.

Regrettably, by recklessly shaving off their hair while destroying the true Dharma, these monks incur a heavy karmic debt. By forgetting that the things of the world are like dreams and mirages, they end up as the servants of noblewomen, which is regrettable. Since they do these things for the sake of the vanities of the world, how will they ever come to honor and respect the experience of the eminently respectable Dharma for the sake of supreme awakening? Their determination to be serious about the Dharma is feeble because the determination to seek the Dharma is imperfect. When they covet valuables, they do not think that those valuables are unobtainable because a woman owns them; when they seek the Dharma, their determination must be even greater. If it is, then even grass, trees, and fences bestow the Dharma; heaven and earth and the myriad things provide the Dharma. This principle should be understood. Even if you have encountered a true teacher, if you have not yet aroused this determination and do not seek the Dharma, you will never be able to bathe in the pure water of the Dharma. You must make a diligent effort.

Also, there are some extremely stupid men nowadays who think, "Women are nothing but sexual objects and providers of food," and they neglect to consider that this kind of thinking results from wrong views. The Buddha's children should not be like this. If you detest women because they are objects of desire, shouldn't you also detest all men? When impure conditions occur, men become objects of desire, women become objects of desire, and those who are neither men nor women become objects of desire. Things in dreams and mirages become objects of desire. Or perhaps reflections in water give rise to impure conduct, or perhaps such conduct occurs as the result of the sun. Spirits become objects of desire, and demons do also. You cannot count all the conditions that produce desire, for it is said that there are eighty-four thousand of them. Aren't all these things to be abandoned? Aren't all of them to be ignored?

The precepts *(vinaya)* say, "The three places of the female and two places of the male are alike completely forbidden." However, if people dislike objects of desire, then all men and women will dislike each other, and in that case they cannot hope for liberation. You must reflect upon this principle in minute detail. Even non-Buddhists may not have wives, but even if they do not, if they do not become Buddhists, they hold wrong views. Among the Buddha's followers the two groups [of laymen and laywomen] have husbands or wives, but even if they do, if they are followers of the Buddha, they do not attempt to equalize heaven and earth [by denying the law of cause and effect].

There are foolish monks in China who vow, "I shall not look at a woman for countless lives to come." What Dharma is this vow based on? Is it the Dharma of ordinary society? Is it the Buddha Dharma? A non-Buddhist Dharma? The Dharma of celestial beings or demons? What demerit is there in femaleness? What merit is there in maleness? There are bad men and good women. If you wish to hear the Dharma and put an end to pain and turmoil, forget about such things as male and female. As long as delusions have not yet been eliminated, neither men nor women have eliminated them; when they are all eliminated and true reality is experienced, there is no distinction of male and female. If you make a vow not to see a woman for ages and ages to come, won't you be neglecting them when you vow, "Sentient beings are numberless; I vow to save them"? If you neglect them, you are no bodhisattva. Is this the great compassion of the Buddha? This vow is the raving of a drunkard who has drunk deeply from the wine barrel of the small vehicle.[7] Neither humans nor celestial beings believe that this conforms to the true teaching.

Moreover, if you hate women because in past lives they violated the precepts, then since all bodhisattvas violated the precepts in past lives, shouldn't you hate them too? If you dislike women on the assumption that they will violate the precepts at some later time, then you must hate all bodhisattvas who have aroused the thought of enlightenment, because they will violate the precepts in some future time. Hating in this manner, you consequently have abandoned everyone. Who will be responsible for manifesting the Buddha Dharma in the world? Your vow is nothing but the crazy words of someone who does not understand the Buddha Dharma. Pitiful! If you make such a vow, you should quietly consider whether all bodhisattvas starting with Śākyamuni have committed wrong acts and whether the thought of enlightenment they aroused is more shallow than your own.

None of the patriarchal teachers who have been associated with the Dharma treasury, and none of the bodhisattvas who dwelt in the world in the Buddha's time, has ever made such a vow, and therefore you should examine carefully whether it is necessary for you to practice and realize the Buddha Dharma. If you make this vow, not only will you not help to liberate women, but if a woman who has experienced the Dharma appears in the world, you will not go and question her when she teaches the Dharma for humans and celestial beings. If you do not go and question her, you are not a bodhisattva; in fact, you are not a Buddhist.

When we look at China, we see monks who seem to have refined their practice for a long time and who know every grain of sand in the ocean [of teachings] but who still flounder in the ocean of life and death. But there are women who visit a teacher, question him, do zazen, and become the teachers of humans and celestials. For instance, there was the old woman who would not sell rice cakes [to a monk] but threw them out instead.[8] It is pitiful, but there are male monks who know every item of doctrine in the scriptures and treatises but who do not see the Buddha Dharma even in a dream.

When you meet someone like this, consider deeply whether he can be enlightened. If you just avoid him as someone to be dreaded, this is the conduct of a disciple of the small vehicle. If you run from the east to take refuge in the west, you will find the same kind of person in the west. Even if you do run away and do not try to clear up his delusions, you will find such men near or far. What is more, to fail to liberate him and run away just deepens his delusion.

There is also something laughable to be found in Japan. There are restricted territories,[9] including Mahayana Buddhist training centers, which are prohibited to nuns and other women. This wrong custom has come down from the distant past and people do not realize that it is wrong. The custom is not changed by experts in legal matters nor is it studied by scholars. It is said to be either the practice of authorities in these matters or the custom of our predecessors, but it is never discussed, and if you laugh at it, it is like a stab in the vitals to others. Who are "authorities"? Are they wise or virtuous? Are they spirits or demons? Have they attained the stage of the ten virtues or the three wisdoms, or the stages of uniform enlightenment or wonderful enlightenment? And if you argue that past customs are not to be changed, does this mean that the endless turning on the wheel of birth and death [which results from past acts] is not to be changed?

Need I mention how perfectly enlightened our great teacher Śākyamuni was? He was enlightened in the way one ought to be enlightened, he practiced what ought to be practiced, and he achieved all the liberations in which one ought to be liberated. Can anyone today even begin to approximate him? Now, in the Buddhist community of his time, there were the four groups consisting of monks, nuns, laymen, and laywomen. There were also the eight groups [of beings outside the human realm], the thirty-seven groups, and the eighty-four thousand groups; all belonged to the Buddha's territory as newly-cultivated fields of the Buddha's community. In any Buddhist restricted territory these days, however, there are no nuns or other females, no eight groups.

We may not hope for a more eminently pure community than that which existed at the time the Tathāgata dwelt in the world. Because this world is inhabited by celestial beings and demons [as well as human beings], the teaching and conversion within the Buddhist assemblies are done without distinction of one's own world or other worlds, or of the worlds of the thousand Buddhas of past, present, and future. If there were any difference in the teaching, you would know that such a place is not a Buddhist assembly.

The four fruits[10] are the ultimate stage. Whether it is the small vehicle or great vehicle, the merits of the ultimate stage are the same. Now, there are many nuns who have acquired the four fruits. Whether it be here in the three realms, in Buddha lands in the ten directions, or in any other world, nuns have reached this stage. Who would hinder their practice [by forbidding them entrance to the restricted territories]? Also, the stage of wonderful enlightenment is the supreme stage.[11] At the time a female became a Buddha,[12] everything in the universe was completely understood. What person would hinder her [from entering the restricted territories], thinking that she had not truly come into this world?

The merits [of her attainment] exist right now, illumining the whole universe, so even though you set up boundary lines, they are of no use.

Also, would you hinder celestial females or demon females from entering? Neither celestial females nor demon females are of a species which can terminate their delusions, and they remain within the cycle of death and rebirth. Sometimes they violate the moral precepts, sometimes they do not. The same is true of human females and animal females; sometimes they violate the precepts, sometimes they do not. Who would get in the way of celestials or demons? They have already visited places where the Buddha taught the Dharma, and they have trained beside the Buddha. Who would believe the Buddha Dharma was the real Dharma if there were a difference of place or a difference of teaching? To believe otherwise is nothing but the extreme stupidity of humans who are still deceived by their delusions and they are more trifling than someone who tries to pull the wool over someone's eyes.

In the ranks of Buddhists, in both the small vehicle and the great vehicle, there are monks, nuns, laymen, and laywomen. This has been known from ancient times among humans and celestial beings. The rank of nun surpasses that of even a great, world-conquering king or that of even Sakra, most powerful of the celestials. Consequently, there is nothing she has not accomplished. How much less can you compare the royalty and courtiers of some small, peripheral country with a nun! Yet we now see restricted territories which are forbidden to nuns but into which go rustics from the rice fields, woodcutters, and others, not to mention royalty, chief ministers of state, other officials, and counselors. If you compare nuns with rice farmers and the others, then what do superior and inferior mean from the standpoint of Buddhist practice and achieving certain ranks? Whether we are talking about worldly usage or Buddhist usage, farmers and others like them should not enter places which are forbidden to nuns. This extreme confusion still persists in this little country of ours. How pitiful that even though the venerable daughters of the compassionate Buddha have come to this small land, they find the doors of some places barred to them.

What is more, those who live in these so-called "restricted territories" do not themselves seem to dread the ten evils and sometimes commit the ten kinds of offense. Living as they do within a place of evil, they should not hate those who do not commit evil. Need I say that they should consider the five unpardonable crimes [one of which consists of harming an arhat] to be very grave? Those who live in the restricted territories should not commit such crimes. Demon territories such as these should be destroyed, and those who live in them ought to learn the Buddha's teaching. They should enter the Buddha's territory. This would be the way to repay the Buddha for his favors.

You predecessors of ours who held such opinions about women, I wonder if you understood the profound idea behind the establishment of Buddhist restricted territories. From whom did you inherit this territory? Who gave you *inka?*

All those which are included in the great territories which were established by the Buddha—Buddhas, ordinary beings, the earth, the sky—are freed from the bonds which tie them to this world, and all return to the root of the wonderful Dharma of all the Buddhas. This being so, all those who once set foot in such a place receive the merits of the Buddha; that is, the merits of a non-relapsing heart and the merits of purity [of body, mouth, and mind].

When one part of the universe is bound to the Dharma, everything in the universe is bound to the Dharma. When one kind is bound to the Dharma, all are bound to it. There are territories bound with water, bound with mind, and bound with space. This territory, it should be understood, has been transmitted through inheritance (from teacher to disciple) over the years. Even after one has sprinkled the body with pure, sweet water, paid reverence by taking the triple refuge, and so on up through cleansing the restricted territory and so on, one should still recite the verse:

> The territory of benevolence pervades the
> whole universe;
> Being just as it is, it is bound to purity.

I wonder whether you predecessors of previous generations understood this deep meaning when you spoke of "restricted territory"? You probably would not understand that within a single restricted territory the whole universe is bound. You should understand that you have been imbibing the wine of the small vehicle and mistakenly think that your meager territory is a large one. I hope some day you will sober up from your intoxication with the wine of delusion and no longer transgress against the all-pervading territory—the great territory—of all the Buddhas. When you try to emancipate all sentient beings and gather them up, they will honor and venerate the merits acquired from teaching and conversion. Then no one will be able to say that you have not acquired the essence of the Way.

## NOTES

1. The word translated as "marrow" here also means "essence," and I have used both translation terms. The allusion is to the tradition according to which Bodhidharma recognized Hui-k'o's attainment by saying that he would receive his marrow or essence. Two other monks and one nun received Bodhidharma's skin, flesh, and bones.

2. The *mondo* exchange was between Hui-neng and some monks. This is case number 29 in the collection of koans named *Mumonkan*.

3. My abbreviated translation of "three virtues and ten wisdoms." These are stages of development according to a scheme taught by the Hua-yen school. In all, there are fifty-three stages, the last three comprising stages of Buddhahood. The ten wisdoms are the ten stages just prior to the

stages of Buddhahood, comprising stages forty-one through fifty. The three vitures are really thirty stages divided up into three groups and comprise stages eleven through forty. In other words, Bodhisattvas in these stages are highly developed in virtue and wisdom.

4. The seven-year-old girl who becomes a Buddha is found in the *Lotus Sutra*. She is identified in the following lines of Dōgen's text.

5. In pre-Mahayana Buddhism, the stage of arhat was considered to be the goal and end of religious practice. The arhat is one who has eliminated all moral and intellectual faults, has ended the round of death and rebirth, understands the four holy truths, and has, in short, completed his or her spiritual training. The Buddha was an arhat as well as being perfectly enlightened.

6. The "four fruits" or "four results" are four stages of spiritual development according to pre-Mahayana Buddhism. In ascending order of perfection they are: "stream-enterer;" "once-returner" (i.e., one who will be reborn in human form one more time); "non-returner" (i.e., one who will not be reborn in human form but will attain the stage of arhat in the world of the celestials); and arhat (see preceeding note).

7. "Small vehicle" refers to pre-Mahayana Buddhism. It is a pejorative name for a form of Buddhism which was considered by Mahayana Buddhism to be exclusive and elitist with respect to who could become an arhat. The small vehicle excluded women in their estimate of who could achieve spiritual perfection, hence Dōgen's criticism.

8. Dōgen's references to a well-known story in the Zen tradition which is found in Mumon's commentary on Case 28 in the *Mumonkan*. Te-shan was a well-known lecturer on the Diamond Sutra. One day in his travels he stopped for refreshments. The word in Chinese which we translate as "refreshment" literally means "to punctuate the mind." The old woman who sold the refreshments said she would give him refreshments if he could tell her what mind it is which is punctuated, since the *Diamond Sutra* says the past mind is unobtainable, present mind is unobtainable, and future mind is unobtainable. The learned Te-shan could not answer, so the old woman threw away the refreshments. Later, in consternation, Te-shan burned all his commentaries and notes on the *Diamond Sutra*.

9. The term I have translated as "restricted territories" (Jap., *kekkai*) refers to precincts or areas, including Buddhist temples and monasteries, which are united or bound to the Dharma. The term literally means "bound territories" or "fixed territories"; i.e., bound or fixed to the Dharma. However, Dōgen's criticism centers on the fact that these places were restricted to all females, whether nuns or laywomen, and I have tried to capture this in my translation.

10. See note six.

11. According to Hua-yen Buddhism, the spiritual path consists of

fifty-two stages, of which the last two are aspects of enlightenment. The fifty-first stage is called "perfect enlightenment" or "uniform enlightenment." The final stage is called "wonderful enlightenment." Dōgen's point, which follows in the text, is that a seven-year-old girl once attained this stage. See following note.

12. The seven-year-old girl who became a perfectly enlightened Buddha is famous in Mahayana Buddhism. The story is told in the *Saddharma-pundarika Sūtra (Lotus Sutra)* in the chapter named "Devadatta."

# SHUNJŪ

*"Spring and Fall"*

A certain monk asked the great master Tung-shan, "When the cold or heat arrives, how can one avoid it?" The master answered, "Why don't you go to a place where there is no cold or heat?" "Where is this place where there is neither cold nor heat?" asked the monk. Said Tung-shan, "When it is cold, the cold kills the monk; when it is hot, the heat kills the monk."

Many people all the way up to the present time have discussed the problem set forth in this dialogue. Nowadays, too, people should exert themselves diligently in solving this problem. The patriarchs have invariably investigated this realm, and those who have investigated it were the patriarchs. In both India and China, many of the Buddhas and patriarchs of past and present have considered the comprehension of this problem to be the actualization of one's [original] face. Actualizing one's [original] face in terms of this problem has been the koan of all the patriarchs.

However, you too must fully clarify the real meaning of that monk's question, "When the cold or heat arrives, how can one avoid it?" It is nothing other than clarifying the problem of the time when cold surely comes or when heat surely comes. What is meant here by "cold" and "heat" is that they are the totality of cold and heat, both are just cold and heat as they really are. Because cold and heat are just that, when they come, they come from the head crown of cold and heat as they really are. They are manifested from the eye pupil of cold and heat just as they really are. This crown of the head is the sphere of cold and heat. Within the pupil of the eye is the place of cold and heat.

Tung-shan's statement, "When it is cold, the cold kills the monk; when it is hot, the heat kills the monk," is a direct hint concerning the arrival of cold and heat. However, even though it is said that when the cold comes, the cold kills, this does not mean you should be trapped by words and think that the heat necessarily kills when it is hot. Therefore, when it is cold, be thoroughly cold, and when it is hot, be thoroughly hot. Though you may try to avoid either one, there is nothing but cold and heat. The cold is the twinkling eyes of the patriarchs, and the heat is the warm flesh of Tung-shan.

The Zen master Ching-yin K'u-mu said this concerning the dialogue between Tung-shan and the monk: "Among many people who practice Zen it is sometimes said that since the monk's question landed him on the side of the conditioned, Tung-shan's answer got him back to the side of non-conditionality. The monk caught the drift of Tung-shan's words and fought his way back towards non-conditionality, and in the face of this development, Tung-shan in turn established himself once more on the side of the conditioned. Conjecturing in this way, they not only blaspheme the Buddha, they land in false views themselves. Haven't you ever heard the words of Chia-shan Shan-hui (Kassan), who said, 'The pleasure of hearing the explanations of ordinary people will grow to such an extent that it will make you ill'? When people with high aspirations to make a sincere effort to practice try to get to the bottom of Tung-shan's words, they will have to understand them by first experiencing enlightenment in his eye and treasury of the true Dharma. Any other teaching of the patriarchs is just the sound of a boiling pot. But still I ask you, in the final analysis, what kind of place is it where there is no cold or heat? Can you tell me? A pair of birds make their nests in the jewelled tower; a pair of mandarin ducks are chained in the golden hall."

Zen Master K'u-mu was in the lineage of Tung-shan, and he was outstanding among the old patriarchal teachers. Many of those involved in training have tended to mistakenly interpret the teachings of Tung-shan from the standpoint of conditionality and non-conditionality, but Master K'u-mu clearly forbade it.[1] If the Buddha's teaching had been transmitted from the limited viewpoint of conditionality and non-conditionality, how would it ever have come down to the present time? However, stray cats and servant girls lacking in experience still do not get to the bottom of Tung-shan's words, and not having ever once experienced the essence of the Buddha, they are completely mistaken and try to guide people by explaining Tung-shan's teaching through the "conditioned," "non-conditioned," and so on, of the "five ranks." However, this is stupid talk, and you must not heed it. Just start at once to study the fact that it is Tung-shan's eye and treasury of the true Dharma.

The Zen master Hung-chih (Wanshi) of Mt. T'ien-lung was a Dharma descendent of the priest Tan-hsia. His posthumous name was Cheng-chüeh. This is what he said about Tung-shan's teaching: "If we try to discuss it,[2] you and I are like a couple of checker players. When you oppose what I have played, I try to defeat you by maneuvering forward and backward. If you understand it in this way, you will understand Tung-shan's real meaning. However, I can not help adding my own explanation to this. When you look at what is within, there is no more cold or heat than there is a drop of water in the ocean right in front of you. What I want to say is that since you can freely stoop over and pluck up the big turtle from the bottom of the ocean, I have to laugh to see you standing on the shore, trying to catch it with a fishing pole." Now, the example of playing checkers is quite appropriate, but what sort of thing is this business of two people playing? If you speak of two people playing, you are still caught in duality [lit., "there will be eight eyes"]. And if you are caught in duality, there is no checker game. How can it be? Therefore, shouldn't it rather be said that only one person is playing checkers and that he is his own opponent? However, with regard to Hung-chih's statement "when you oppose me," you should ponder this with your hearts and bodies. The meaning of "when you oppose me" is that you are thoroughly you and already there is no one called "me" here. Do not overlook the significance of "I try to defeat you." This is just muddiness of mind. The hiker washes his feet and he washes the tassels of his shoes. This is also like a jewel within a jewel. When it gleams, it illuminates others and it illuminates itself.

The Zen master Huan-wu (K'e-ch'in, known in Japan as Kokugon) of Mt. Chia said, "The container makes the jewel run about and the jewel runs about within the container. There is the unconditioned within the conditioned and the conditioned within the unconditioned. It is like an antelope sleeping with his antlers hanging from tree branches so as not to leave any clues as to where he is, and the hunting dog searches in vain in the forest for his location." The expression "the container makes the jewel run about" is a marvel of past and present times and is beyond comparison. In the past it was explained as meaning that the jewel which runs about in the vessel never stops looking. However, the antelope now hangs his antlers from the sky, and the forest is searching for the dog.

Zen Master Ming-chiao (Secchō) was the disciple of Chih-men Kuang-tsu. His posthumous name was Chung-hsien. He said, "This teaching kindly extended to the monk is as inaccessible as a ten-thousand-fathom cliff, and it is not restricted to conditioned and unconditioned. The old hill of lapis lazuli is illuminated by the moon, and the dog who howls at the moon vainly runs up the stairs of the old hall." Ming-chiao was in the third generation after Yün-men and it can be said that he cultivated the Way sufficiently. His expression, "This teaching kindly extended to the monk is as inaccessible as a ten-thousand-fathom cliff," may be said to reveal the incomparable realm, but this is not necessarily so.

Now, the circumstance of the monk's question and Tung-shan's answer neither speaks of "teaching" nor does it not speak of it; the Buddha is not said to appear in the world nor not to appear. How much less does it speak of "conditioned" and "unconditioned"! If you do not use such expressions as "conditioned" and "non-conditioned," you will cease to be unskillful with Tung-shan's koan. You will never reach his realm if you do not use all your powers to penetrate the truth. Therefore, study this with all your strength, and stop saying that Tung-shan's teaching can be understood by means of the "conditioned" and "non-conditioned" of the "five ranks", when there is no excuse for it.

The Zen master Ch'ang-ling (Shou-cho) said, "There is the non-conditioned within the conditioned and the conditioned within the non-conditioned, and they pervade the human world eternally. However often you may wish to return to the place where there is no cold or heat, you still cannot return. The grass grows abundantly before the gate as it has since olden times." Now, although Ch'ang-ling is speaking to you about the conditoned and non-conditioned, he is just using them as the state of reality. It is not that they cannot be used in connection with reality, for if this were the case, how could there be this "exists within the conditioned"?

The priest Ta-wei Fa-hsing said, "Tung-shan's answer pervades that place where there is no cold or heat, and he does this for your sake. The withered tree produces a single blossom. It is laughable to watch a person tearing apart the boat looking for the sword which fell into the water. Right now, he abides in the cold ashes."[3] These words freely go a little beyond Tung-shan's koan.

The Zen master Chan-t'ang Wen-chun said, "When it is cold, everything is thoroughly cold; when it is hot, everything is thoroughly hot. Heat and cold originally have no connection. Running all over heaven and earth looking into mundane matters, the noble lord accepts a vulgar crown for his head." I would like to ask Chan-t'ang just what sort of thing is this "no connection"? Quickly, quickly, answer!

The Zen master Fo-teng (Shou-chün) said, "Tung-shan's teaching about the place where there is no cold or heat is a source of great delusion for monks without experience. If you move towards the fire when it is cold and cool yourself when it is hot, you will be able to avoid cold and heat for your whole life." Now, this Shou-chün was a teacher in the lineage of Wu-tsu Fa-yen, but his words are the words of a baby. However, the words "you will be able to avoid cold and heat for your whole life" contain in them the potential for revealing a deep meaning. "Whole life" means "the totality of life." "Avoiding cold and heat" means "dropping off mind and body."

All these critical verses up to now by patriarchal teachers of various times have tried to explain Tung-shan's statement, but they still fail to penetrate Tung-shan's realm. The reason for this is that in their everyday lives, these patriarchal teachers did not really understand what cold and heat are, and so they spoke of either moving closer to a fire or cooling oneself. What a shame! I wonder if you, Shou-chün, studied the matter of what cold and heat are? How sad that the Way of the Buddha has become completely lost!

You should make a koan of Tung-shan's statement, and make it your own problem, and so come to understand the meaning of cold and heat, experience the time of cold and heat, and use cold and heat as your own. If you still do not understand it, you should reflect upon yourself and consider your own past wickedness. Even people who are not Buddhists understand time, and there are holy people and wise people who can explain the myriad things, and even wise people and fools are able to explain them. Do not explain the cold and heat which are a problem in Buddhism as being like the cold and heat as understood by foolish people. At any rate, just study the problem earnestly.

## NOTES

1. The terms "conditoned" and "non-conditioned" in this passage and later on in an essay are my attempt to translate the terms *p'ien* and *cheng,* both of which are key terms in Tung-shan's well known "five ranks." The expression *p'ien chung cheng* refers to the first rank, which may be translated as "the non-conditioned within the conditioned." *Cheng chung p'ien,* which is the second rank, means "the conditioned within the non-conditioned." Other terms might be substituted; *cheng* means "correct," "upright," "principle," "true," and so on. *P'ien* means "partial," "inclined," "one-sided," and so on. As contraries, they can also be seen in terms of *li* and *shih,* emptiness and form, the absolute and determined, and so on, and this fundamental Chinese pattern of thinking forms the basis of the discussion in *Shunjū.* A discussion of Tung-shan's "five ranks" may be found in Heinrich Dumoulin's *History of Zen Buddhism,* and in Charles Luk's *Ch'an and Zen Teaching: Second Series.*

2. The "it" referred to here, according to the commentaries, may be either the "five ranks" system, or the problem which forms the substance of the koan.

3. According to the commentaries, "dry ashes" refers to the vehicle of the *srāvakas* and *pratyekabuddhas,* which are referred to by Mahayana Buddhists as the "two vehicles." The reference seems to be to the tendency of the two vehicles to make a sharp distinction between samsara and nirvana, a distinction denied by Mahayana Buddhism in general, and by Dōgen in particular. The important question in this essay is precisely that of "Where is there to be found that place where one is free from birth and death?" Dōgen's comments make it clear that it is this very realm of birth and death.

# SHINJIN INGA

*"Deep Faith in Cause and Effect"*

Whenever the Zen master Pai-chang (Ta-chih Huai-hai) preached the Dharma in the Dharma hall, there was always an old man there who respectfully listened to the Dharma teaching and then left with the monks. However, one day, when the monks left, he stayed behind. "Who is this standing before me?" asked the master. The old man answered, "I am not really a human being. Long, long ago, during the time of Kāśyapa Buddha, I lived here as chief priest of a monastery. One day, a monk asked me, 'Does a person who has perfected his training and is enlightened become subject to cause and effect or not?' I answered, 'He is not subject to cause and effect.' And because of this answer, I have spent five hundred lifetimes in the body of a fox. I now ask you respectfully to say some word which will change my mental attitude[1] and free me from this fox body." Then he asked the master, "Is a person who has become enlightened subject to the law of cause and effect?" Pai-chang replied, "He does not ignore

159

cause and effect." Upon hearing these words, the old man had a great satori. Bowing to Pai-chang, he said, "I am now liberated from the body of the fox, which you will find at the foot of the cliff near the monastery. May I be so bold as to request the Chief Priest to have it buried as you would a dead monk?"

The master had the *weina* (*ino*) strike the mallet and announce to the monks that there would be a funeral service for a dead monk right after the meal. The monks were quite agitated and wondered, "Since all the monks here in this monastery are healthy and there is no one in the infirmary, who could have died, that we must perform funeral services for a dead monk?" After they had eaten, the master took them to the foot of the cliff where, poking about with his staff, he found the remains of a fox. He had the body cremated in accordance with the custom among Buddhists.

That evening, during his talk in the Dharma hall, he spoke of the circumstances centering around the cremation of the fox. Huang-po asked him, "The old man gave a wrong answer to the monk, and as a consequence, he had to abide in the body of a fox for five hundred lifetimes. But if he had not made a mistake, what would he have become?" Pai-chang said, "Come closer and I'll tell you." Huang-po came close to the master and suddenly slapped him on the cheek. Pai-chang clapped his hands and laughed. "I thought the foreigner's beard was red, but it was really a red-bearded foreigner." This story is recorded in the *T'ien-sheng huang teng lu*.[2]

Monks in training do not understand the principle of cause and effect and consequently many have made the mistake of thoughtlessly doubting this principle. This is truly lamentable, for once bad habits begin to spread in the world, the Way of the patriarchs begins to gradually decline. To think that one is not subject to cause and effect is to deny cause and effect, and the result is that you fall into the bad destinations of animals, the purgatories, and so on.

However, to affirm this great principle and say that one

does not ignore cause and effect clearly indicates a deep faith in the principle of cause and effect. As a result, one can become liberated from suffering in this present lifetime. Do not have any doubt about the principle of cause and effect. Do not question it. Many who practice Zen these days do doubt it. How do I know they doubt it? They either believe that they are not subject to cause and effect, or else they believe the nature of this principle is such that no one can escape it anyway, so in either case, they deny cause and effect.

The nineteenth patriarch, Kumārata, said, "There are three periods for the maturation of good and bad karma.[3] When we look at human life, we see that often the compassionate person suffers and dies, while the wicked person who gets along in the world by means of violence is happy and lives a long life. Also, the decent person is unhappy and wretched, while the wicked person who commits the five unpardonable offenses[4] without ever thinking twice about it is happy. This is the way it seems, and we may wonder why it is this way. When we study this situation, we see that the person who trains in a superficial way thinks that cause and effect have nothing to do with this life and that misery and happiness have nothing to do with cause and effect. This person does not understand that the law of cause and effect never deviates, any more than a shadow or echo deviates from its source. Nor does he understand that the law of cause and effect never lapses, even after millions of eons."

You should understand that none of the patriarchs has ever denied the law of cause and effect. It is due to their own negligence that people who practice Zen these days do not understand the teachings of the compassionate patriarchs. Negligent though they may be, they become self-styled teachers of men and gods, and thus they rob men and gods and are the sworn enemies of all real students. These fellows who crowd around younger students should not spread the false teaching that denies the principle of cause and effect. It is a wrong teaching because it is not the Dharma of the patriarchs. If you become careless, you will fall utterly into this wrong view.

Certain monks in Sung China these days say, "We have acquired human form and have encountered the Dharma, but we still do not understand this present life or the future life. We understand that after that priest became a fox, he spent five hundred lifetimes in the body of a fox, but he did not become a fox as the result of karma. Even though he passed through the difficult barrier of practice and acquired supreme enlightenment, he did not remain in that state, but descended into the world of animals and was constantly reborn there."

This is the sort of thing taught by people who are called "great leaders of the world." But this explanation is not in accordance with the essence of the patriarchs. There are those who have the supernatural power to know their past lives, whether as humans, animals, or some other form of sentient life. However, this supernatural power is not acquired by becoming enlightened in the Dharma, but is rather the result of bad karma in past lives. Sākyamuni himself taught this principle extensively. That people do not understand it is due to their neglect of practice. Truly it is a shame, for even though one knows a thousand past lives or even ten thousand past lives, it is not really the Dharma. Even non-Buddhists sometimes know the events of eighty thousand eons. However, it is still not the Dharma. Even if you can understand the events of five hundred lifetimes a little, it is not really much of an ability.

Zen monks in China nowadays display a dismal ignorance of the fact that this teaching of not being subject to cause and effect is an incorrect teaching. What a pity! While they are worthy of the Buddha's teaching which is correctly transmitted from patriarch to patriarch, they become those fellows who negate the law of cause and effect. Those who practice Zen should stir themselves and clarify this principle of cause and effect right now. Pai-chang's assertion that one does not ignore cause and effect clarifies this principle. Therefore, the principle according to which one acquires a certain result on the basis of a cause in the form of action is quite clear, and it is the truth of the Buddha and patriarchs. Generally speaking, if you have still not sufficiently clarified the Buddha Dharma, you ought not to preach the Dharma rashly and heedlessly to others.

Nāgārjuna, our patriarchal teacher,[5] said, "The non-Buddhists say that if you deny the law of cause and effect in this life, then the present life and the future life are destroyed. If you deny that the appearance of all the Buddhas in the world due to their enlightenment results from cause and effect, then you negate the Three Jewels, the four holy truths, and the four fruits of the monk." You must clearly understand that if you deny cause and effect in the world or in the supramundane realm, you have become a non-Buddhist. Saying, "The present world does not exist," you believe that while the body appears here in this world, the self abides in a permanent, immutable world. The self is identified with the mind. The mind is explained as something remaining apart from the body. This is the way in which non-Buddhists think about the body.

Or else it is sometimes said that when a person dies, his self returns to the great ocean of essence. Therefore, if one naturally returns to the ocean of essence even though he has not cultivated the Dharma, he no longer transmigrates in the world of birth and death, and therefore there is no afterworld. This is the annihilationist view of non-Buddhists. Even if in appearance he looks like a Buddhist monk, this fool who believes such a teaching is not at all a son of the Buddha. He is truly a non-Buddhist. The idea that the present world and the afterworld do not exist because there is no law of cause and effect is incorrect. The denial of cause and effect results from not studying with a real teacher. If you study for a long time with a real teacher, you will not fall into wrong views which deny cause and effect. You should deeply believe in the compassionate teaching of Nāgārjuna and humbly accept it.

The great master Hsüan-chüeh (Yung-chia Chen-chüeh) was a prominent disciple of Zen Master Ts'ao-ch'i. Earlier, he had studied the *Lotus Sutra* of the T'ien-t'ai sect, and he was a fellow student of the great master Tso-chi Hsüan-lang. When Hsüan-chüeh read the *Nirvāna Sūtra,* a golden light filled his room. When this happened, Hsüan-chüeh was enlightened in the principle of the Birthless. Thereupon, he continued his efforts, and he visited the Zen master Hui-neng on Mt. Ts'ao-ch'i and demonstrated his enlightenment to the Sixth Patriarch. Hui-neng approved his satori and transmitted the Dharma to him. Afterward, Hsüan-chüeh composed the *Cheng tao ko.* In it are these lines:

> A liberal emptiness negates cause and
>     effect;
> Like flourishing grasses and rippling
>     waves, calamities come.

You should understand that if you deny cause and effect, you will invite calamity. All the old Buddha patriarchs clarified the matter of cause and effect. However, Zen monks nowadays who come after them are deluded about cause and effect. In this state of affairs, people who arouse a pure thought of enlightenment and attempt to study the Dharma for the sake of the Dharma should clarify the principle of cause and effect in the same way the old patriarchs did. "No cause, no effect" is something said by non-Buddhists.

The Zen master Hung-chih Cheng-chüeh (Wanshi) explained Pai-chang's statement about cause and effect with these verses from his *Ts'ung yung lu:*

> A foot of water becomes a foot of waves;
> So nothing could be done about the 500
>     lives as a fox.
> Arguing 'is not subject to causation' or 'does
>     not ignore it,'

As of old, they still fall into a den of
  complexities and cannot escape.
Ha-ha-ha! I wonder if you understand?
O monks, if you have eliminated false
  thoughts and are free,
You will have no difficulty with my
  [mindless] 'goo-goo, nah-nah'!
Sing before the spirits and dance with the
  earth deities
And you will be able to compose your own
  tune.
Then you and I, united, will clap hands
  joyously,
Singing 'tum-tiddly-um tum-tiddly-um
  tum.'

Now Hung-chih's phrase "Arguing 'is not subject to causation' or 'does not ignore it,' they still fall into a den of complexities" means nothing less than that not being subject to cause and effect and not ignoring cause and effect are to be considered to be the same.

At any rate, this principle of cause and effect is still not thoroughly clear. The reason is that even though it is a fact that the old man was freed from the body of the fox, it did not say that after being freed he was reborn in the human world, or that he was reborn in the celestial realm, or in the realm of animals, and so on. If after leaving the body of the fox he had been reborn in one of the fortunate destinations, he would have become a human or a celestial being. If he had been reborn in an evil destination, he would have been reborn in the purgatories, among hungry spirits, as an animal, or as a fighting *asura*. When he was freed from the body of the fox, he had to be reborn someplace. If you say that upon dying a living being returns to the great ocean of essential being, nirvana, or that he returns to the Great Self, that is the incorrect view of non-Buddhists.

165

The Zen master Chia-shan Yüan-wu (Kassan) explained the situation in the following verses:

> When a fish swims, the water becomes
>     muddied;
> When a bird flies, its feathers fall.
> Just as an object is reflected in a polished
>     mirror,
> Nothing can escape the law of cause and
>     effect.
> Just as not a single thing can be hidden in
>     the vast sky,
> The five hundred lives as a fox came from
>     the great activity of cause and effect.
> Swift lightning may rend the mountains,
>     the winds may make the seas tremble.
> But just as gold refined a hundred times
>     still retains its color,
> The activity of cause and effect is eternal
>     and unchanging.

In these verses, there is some remnant of the tendency to deny cause and effect, and there is also some remainder of the eternalist view.

> The Zen master Ching-shan Ta-hui says,
> The turning phrases 'is not subject' and
>     'does not ignore' are identical
> In the same way a stone head and the earth
>     spirit are the same.
> The freedom from the fox body after five
>     hundred lives
> Was like the pulverizing of a silver
>     mountain.
> Someone hears such a doctrine and claps
>     his hands joyously
> And with shaking belly laughs
>     uproariously—it is Pu-tai[6]

People in China in the present time consider these men to be splendid teachers. However, Ta-hui's opinion is still far from the teaching of skillful means, for it falls into the view of naturalness held by non-Buddhists and does not exemplify a deep faith in cause and effect.

All in all, more than thirty priests have composed verses or koans in connection with Pai-chang's fox, but every one of them thought that the words "is not subject to cause and effect" denies the law of cause and effect. What a pity! These men did not clarify the principle of cause and effect, and while they argue "does" or "does not," they fruitlessly waste their lives in the very midst of life. In studying the Dharma, the first thing to do is to clarify the principle of cause and effect. The kind of people who deny it produce extremely bad wrong views and cut off the roots of goodness and end up as people who are hard to help.

The principle of cause and effect is clear, and it is evident everywhere. The person who does evil falls into the purgatories, and the person who cultivates good is freed from all suffering, and this truth never varies by so much as an inch. If this principle were destroyed, the Buddhas would not appear in the world, and Bodhidharma would not have gone to China. Therefore, living beings would not see the Buddha or hear the Dharma. The principle of cause and effect cannot be explained by such people as Confucius and Lao-tzu; only the Buddhas and patriarchs have explained it and correctly transmitted it. Zen students during the time of the decline of the Dharma[7] are unhappy and can not find a real teacher, and consequently, they cannot hear the real Dharma. Thus, they cannot come to clearly understand the principle of cause and effect. Moreover, if they deny this principle, then as a result of their offense, they cannot avoid the calamities which befall them as numerous as blades of grass in the fields. Even though one commits no other bad karma besides denying cause and effect, the pain which comes from just this one wrong view is extremely great.

Therefore, those who study Zen in the Buddha Dharma may wish to start by arousing the thought of enlightenment and repaying the kindness of the Buddha and patriarchs, but first of all they should clearly understand the principle of cause and effect.

## NOTES

1. The phrase I have translated here as "a word to change one's mental attitude" is literally "turning word" in the Japanese. It is a technical expression in Zen, referring to the appropriate words or expressions uttered by a Zen master in confrontation with a disciple, for the purpose of causing a mental "turning" or transformation. Pai-chang's answer to the old man is an example. Usually in Zen literature, these "turning words" are followed by the statement that the disciple had a satori.

2. This is also case number two in the well-known collection of koans, *Mumonkan*.

3. According to classical Buddhist thought, the fruit or results of karma can occur during three periods. Some karma bears its results in the present life, sometimes as soon as a morally charged act is performed. However, the effects of the act may not occur until the next life. In some cases, many more lifetimes may lapse before the effects of the karma are felt. Thus, it may seem that the wicked flourish and the innocent suffer sometimes, but this is just the maturation of past good and bad karma.

4. The five unpardonable offenses are 1: killing one's father; 2: killing one's mother; 3: killing an arhat; 4: creating a schism in the Sangha; 5: causing a Buddha to bleed. There can be no expiation for these offenses, and the offender falls immediately into one of the drearier Buddhist hells.

5. Nāgārjuna is counted as one of the Indian patriarchs of the Zen lineage.

6. Pu-tai (Jap. Hotei) is a fat, jolly character in dishevelled clothes, carrying a large, bulging sack, who is often portrayed in Chinese Zen paintings. He is the so-called "laughing Buddha" often seen in souvenir and gift shops. He is thought to have been a real person who was considered by the folk to be an earthly incarnation of Maitreya Buddha. It is interesting that here he is portrayed as a non-Buddhist.

7. Dōgen is alluding to the widely held view that the Buddha Dharma had entered the last of three periods of change. The first period

(often given as 500 years) was supposedly the period of the authentic Dharma, during which time monks and nuns really practiced hard and led lives in accordance with the Buddha's teaching. The next period is called the period of the "counterfeit Dharma," when monks look like monks but do not really observe the teaching in a strict manner. The third period, called *mappō* in Japan, was thought to have started near the end of the eleventh century, and marked the utter collapse of the Dharma. At this time, there would not even be any pretense of following the Dharma, and it would be a period of moral, social, and religious degeneracy. Dōgen apparently accepted the theory of *mappō*, but he seems to have drawn different conclusions than Shinran, founder of Pure Land Buddhism.

# NYORAI ZENSHIN

*"The Tathāgata's Whole Body"*

On one occasion when the Buddha was staying at the Vulture Peak in Rājagriha, he spoke to the bodhisattva, the mahāsattva, Bhaisajya-rāja: "O Bhaisajya-rāja, in every lifetime you should discuss, read, recite, and copy this sutra, and wherever this sutra is found, you should build a stupa higher and broader than all the others, adorned with the seven precious stones. But you should not place the relics of the Buddha within it. Why? Because the whole body of the Tathagata is already within it. Therefore, this stupa should be honored, revered, and praised with offerings of flowers, incense, jewels, canopies, banners, music, and songs. When people see this stupa, and pay homage to it and honor it, all these people, you should know, will be close to supreme bodhi."[1] What is spoken of here as the "sutra" is "discussion, reading, chanting, and copying." The mark of ultimate reality which all things have[2] is also the sutra. As for the "stupa which one should build of the seven precious stones," the stupa is also

171

the mark of ultimate reality of all things. The size of this extremely tall and broad stupa is the size of the mark of ultimate reality which all things have [that is to say, it is markless]. "The whole body of the Tathagata is already within the stupa" means that the sutra is the whole body.

Therefore, discussing the sutra, reading it, chanting it, copying it, and so on, are themselves the whole body of the Tathagata. You should honor, revere, and praise it with flowers, incense, jewels, canopies, banners, music, and songs. It is said that one should honor, revere, and praise it with heavenly flowers, heavenly incense, heavenly canopies, and so on. All these are the mark of ultimate reality which all things have. But they can also be the very best flowers, the best incense, the best robes, the best clothing, and so on, of the human world. All these are also the mark of ultimate reality. Honoring and revering are all the mark of ultimate reality. You should understand that when it is said that a stupa should be built but that the Tathagata's relics should not be placed in it, what is meant is that the sutra is the relics of the Tathāgata; it is the Tathagata's whole body. There are no greater merits than those of directly hearing the golden words of the Buddha when he preaches the Dharma. [The Sutra itself is the direct sound of the golden words; they are the Buddha's whole body.] You should accumulate merits as fast as you can and be diligent in heaping them up [by reading, chanting, and copying the sutras which are worthy of honor, reverence, and praise]. If there are people who honor and revere this stupa, you should understand that this is "all are close to *anuttara samyak sambodhi.*"[3] When beings see this stupa, they should sincerely pay homage to it and revere it. They will be close to anuttara samyak sambodhi. This "close" has nothing to do with intervals such as close or far; it is the anuttara samyak sambodhi which we may say "all are close to." When we now see this sutra received and upheld, read and recited, understood, preached, and copied, "we can see the stupa." It is delightful that "all are close to anuttara samyak sambodhi."

This being so, the sutra is the whole body of the Tathagata. Paying homage to the sutra is paying homage to the Tathagata. Coming into contact with the sutra is meeting the Tathagata. The sutra is the Buddha's relics. This being so, the relics are this sutra. Even though you may understand that this sutra is the relics of the Buddha, if you do not know that the relics are the sutra, it cannot be said that you know the Buddha Way yet. The mark of reality of all things in the present time is the sutra. The human world, the heavens, the realms of the sea and space, other realms, all are the mark of ultimate reality. They are the sutra; they are the bone relics.

You should receive and support, read and recite, explain, preach, and copy the bone relics, and in so doing become enlightened. This is being in accord with the sutra. There are relics of ancient Buddhas, relics of Buddhas of the present time, relics of śravakas and pratyekabuddhas, relics of world rulers, and relics of the kings of lions. There are also the relics of wooden Buddhas, relics of Buddhas painted on silk, and there are human relics. Nowadays in Sung China, the relics of Buddhas and patriarchs who lived at various times appear. There have been many relics which have appeared after the Buddhas and patriarchs have died. All are the sutra.

Śākyamuni Buddha once spoke to a great crowd, saying "The life-duration which I acquired from the merits of my originally practicing the path of the bodhisattva is eternal and not yet terminated."[4] The eight *koki* and four *shō*[5] of relics which now remain are the Buddha's life. The life span resulting from the merits of the original bodhisattva practices is not limited in size to even such things as the size of the universe and so on; it transcends this limit, it is limitless. This is the whole body of the Tathagata, it is this sutra.

The bodhisattva Jnānākara said, "I see that even though for countless eons Śākyamuni Buddha has practiced difficult and painful practices, accumulated merits, and sought the Way of the bodhisattva, and that even though he is now a

Buddha, he still practices diligently. I see that in all worlds, from those the size of the whole universe down to those the size of a mustard seed, there is no place the bodhisattva does not abandon his own body and life in order to help living beings. All this is done for the sake of living beings, and afterwards he will achieve perfect enlightenment."[6]

You should clearly understand that this universe is a fragment of the red heart, and space is contained within the hollow of the hand. They are the whole body of the Tathagata. This has nothing to do with the Buddha's renouncing his body or not renouncing his body. The relics of the Buddha are neither prior to his appearance in the world nor do they come after his disappearance, for it is not really a question of whether they are or are not the Buddha. The long eons of difficult and painful practices are the activity of the womb of the Buddha, they are the activity of the innermost being of the Buddha; that is to say, they are the Buddha's skin, flesh, bone, and marrow. When it is said that these practices have not ceased even for a second, it means that even though he is perfectly enlightened, he still practices vigorously, and he continues forever even though he converts the whole universe. This activity is the whole body of the Tathagata.

## NOTES

1. The quote is from the *Lotus Sutra*, "Dharma Teacher" chapter. All references to "sutra" in this essay mean *Lotus Sutra*.

2. "Mark of ultimate reality which all things have" is a translation of *jissō*, sometimes translated as "true-mark" or "mark of reality" in other translations. It means that all things just as they are reveal the true state of reality, the body of the Buddha.

3. *Anuttara samyak sambodhi* means "supreme, perfect enlightenment." It is the enlightenment of Śākyamuni.

4. *Lotus Sutra*, chapter named "Life-Duration."

5. These are volume measures, a *koku* equalling almost five gallons, a *shō* equalling a little over one and a half quarts.

6. Also a quotation from the *Lotus Sutra*.

# GYŌJI

*"Continuous Practice"*

In the great Way of the Buddha patriarchs there is always supreme continuous practice which is the Way without beginning or end. Arousing the thought of enlightenment, practice, bodhi, and nirvana have not the slightest break, but are continuous practice which goes on forever. Therefore, it is neither one's own effort nor someone else's effort; it is pure, continuous practice which transcends the opposition of self and others.

The merit of this continuous practice upholds oneself and others, because due to one's own effort, all worlds in the universe all the way up to the heavenly abodes immediately share in its benefits. Even though you may not be aware of it yourself and others are not aware of it, that is the way it is. Therefore, because of the continuous practice of all the Buddhas and patriarchs, our own continuous practice becomes a reality and the Way of the Buddhas is opened for us. Because of our own continuous practice, the continuous practice of all the Buddhas and patriarchs is manifested, and the Way of all the Buddhas is opened. Because of our own continuous practice, there are the merits of the Way which is without beginning. Because of this continuous practice, each former Buddha and patriarch abides as a Buddha, transcends Buddhahood, is resolved as a Buddha, and is perfected as a Buddha endlessly.

Because of this continuous practice, there are sun, moon, and stars. Because of this continuous practice, there are earth, sky, and heart within and body without, the four elements and the five skandhas. Continuous practice is not something ordinary people are fond of, but nevertheless, it is the true refuge for everyone. Because of this continuous practice of the Buddhas of past, present, and future, the Buddhas of past, present, and future are manifested. The merits of this continuous practice are sometimes not hidden, and so beings arouse the thought of enlightenment and begin to practice. Sometimes these merits of continuous practice are not evident, and so beings do not see and hear them and do not come to understand them. But you should understand that even though these merits are not revealed, they are not concealed.

When the continuous practice which manifests itself is truly continuous practice, you may be unaware of what circumstances are behind it, and the reason why you do not notice them is that to understand such a thing is not that special. Conditional arising is continuous practice, but continuous practice is not conditionally generated, and this you should diligently seek to understand. It is this way because continuous practice is not dominated by any other thing. This kind of continuous practice which reveals continuous practice is nothing more than our continuous practice now. The immediate "now" of continuous practice is not something which existed in me from before. The time called "now" is not born from continuous practice. The time when continuous practice is manifested is what we call "now." Consequently, one day of continuous practice by us becomes the seed of all the Buddhas; it is the continuous practice of all the Buddhas. On the basis of this continuous practice, all the Buddhas are manifested. Not to continuously practice what is to be continuously practiced is to hate the Buddha, not to venerate the Buddha, to hate continuous practice, not to be born with the Buddha and die with the Buddha, not to learn with the Buddha, and not to practice with the Buddha. Opening up enlightenment in this present time and letting go of enlightenment are the action of continuous practice. Becoming a Buddha and transcending Buddhahood are the action of continuous practice.

For this reason, you may sometimes try to conceal the deluded thought of trying to avoid continuous practice when you neglect it by saying that "even avoiding continuous practice is itself continuous practice," but this is a half-hearted continuous practice, and it cannot be considered to be seeking continuous practice. Truly, it is like a poor person throwing away his inheritance and wandering off to some other land. Even though when you are distressed the wind and rain do not rob you of life and body, still the paternal inheritance will be lost. Therefore, continuous practice should never be neglected for even a second.

Our compassionate father and great teacher, Śākyamuni Buddha, went into the mountains when he was nineteen and began continuous practice, and at the age of thirty, he engaged in continuous practice which perfected his practice along with that of the earth and all sentient beings. Up to the age of eighty, he practiced continuously in the mountains or in monasteries. He never returned to the palace of his father or resumed his position as a prince. For his whole life he never wore new monks' robes or had a new alms bowl. Not for a day, not for a moment, was he ever alone, but constantly taught others and received them in the Dharma. He did not ever reject the veneration of humans or divine beings, nor was he ever upset at abuse from the followers of other teachings. The teaching and conversion activities of his whole lifetime were nothing but continuous practice. Keeping his robes clean and begging for his food were nothing but continuous practice.

The eighth patriarch, Mahākāśyapa, was Śākyamuni's heir. In a previous life he had engaged in the practice of the twelve austerities as his continuous practice, and he was never negligent. The twelve austerities are as follows:

1. He did not accept invitations to eat at the homes of laymen, but every day he begged his food, and he did not eat the remains of the monks' one daily meal.

2. He lived in the mountains and never stayed in peoples' houses, counties, prefectures, or villages.

3. He did not beg for robes when he met people, nor did he take them if they were offered. He took the clothes off dead bodies, mended them, and wore them.

4. He stayed in fields and beneath trees.

5. He ate one meal a day.

6. He did not sleep on a broad bed. He continued to sit, and if he grew sleepy he walked around.

7. He owned only the three robes and did not use bedding.

8. He lived on the sides of hills, not in temples, and he did not live among people. He did zazen while gazing at the bones of the dead, always seeking the truth.

9. He wished only to be by himself and did not want to be with people. Also, he did not sleep among others.

10. When he had eaten some fruits and nuts, he would eat some rice, and then he

would eat no more.

11. He desired to live only in wild places, and he never stayed in huts under the trees.

12. He ate neither meat nor dairy products, nor did he ever rub hemp oil on his body.

These are the twelve austerities. He observed them faithfully for a whole lifetime, never backsliding. Even after he inherited the eye and treasury of the true Dharma from the Buddha, he never gave up the observance of these austerities. Once the Buddha remarked, "You are already quite old, please eat the regular monk's food as well as nuts and fruit." Mahākāśyapa replied, "If you had not appeared in the world, I would have been a pratyekabuddha[1] dwelling alone in mountains and forests. Now, because you have appeared in the world, I have acquired the nourishment of the truth. In order to observe continuous practice, I will not eat monk's food." The Buddha praised him for this.

Also, Mahākāśyapa once grew quite emaciated because of his austerities, and when some monks saw him, they made fun of him. The Buddha courteously sat Mahākāśyapa beside him on his own seat. So Mahḳāśyapa sat on the same seat with the Buddha. He was the elder member of the Buddha's order, and all the circumstances of his whole lifetime of continuous practice can not be completely told.

For his whole life, the tenth patriarch, Pārśva, did not rest his ribs on the ground in order to lie down. Such practices, even though they continued until he was eighty, culminated in enlightenment and becoming a patriarchal teacher. Because he did not foolishly waste time, in three short years of intense effort he came to correctly transmit the Dharma treasury of the true teaching of enlightenment. This honored one was in his mother's womb for sixty years, and when he was born he already had white hair. He was called the "Rib Saint" because he vowed never to lie down, but rested only on an armrest. In the dark his hands emitted flashes of light, which he used to help him read the scriptures and treatises. He exhibited these paranormal powers which he possessed naturally. Now when the Rib Saint was eighty, he renounced the world and made his home departure. However, some young people in the city criticized this, saying, "You are just a senile old man. How did you get to be so stupid? Those who make their home departure do two things: they practice zazen and chant the scriptures. Now that you are so old, you must not behave in this manner any more. You left home and joined the Buddha's order only in order to get something to eat." The Rib Saint heard their criticism, thanked them, and made this vow: "If I do not master the three parts of the canon, cut off all the desires of the three realms, and obtain the six paranormal powers, and make the eight liberations my own,[2] I will never use an armrest." From then on, he was careful about time, and even if he was walking about, he meditated, so that every day he was engaged in meditation whether he was sitting, doing things, going out, or returning. In the daytime, he did walking meditation, sitting meditation, and studied the scriptures, and at night, he did sitting meditation, so day and night for three years without a break he maintained his continuous practice. Consequently, he mastered the three parts of the canon,[3] cut off the desires of the three worlds,[4] and acquired the power of the three lores of the arhat.[5] When others heard of this, they praised him and called him the Rib Saint.

The Rib Saint was born after being in the womb for sixty years. I wonder if he didn't practice intensely while still in the womb? After he was born, when he reached eighty, he aroused the thought of enlightenment and made his home departure for the first time. From the time he was conceived, it was 140 years. Truly, he was a rare, outstanding man of talent. He was older than any of his Dharma contemporaries, for he had grown old in the womb, and he continued to grow old after he was born. However, he took people's criticism to heart when he left the home life, and because he achieved the intention of his vow of home departure and acquiring the Way, after three years his practice was completed. No one who tries to do this sort of thing will speak unkindly of his example. Do not think ill of those who are very old.

It is difficult to investigate this life of ours or to thoroughly comprehend it. Is it life, or is it not life? Is it old age, or is it not old age? In accordance with different viewpoints, they are not at all identical, and the viewpoints themselves differ according to the individual's environment and abilities. If you want to understand such things, be determined and diligent in your practice. You should understand that life and death in their true form exist only within your practice, and that your diligent practice does not exist within life and death. Nowadays, when people reach the age of fifty, or sixty, or seventy, or eighty, they stop practicing, which is the limit of stupidity. No matter how many years you have lived up to now, they are nothing but thoughts in your mind, and you do not understand them in terms of practice. Do not look back on these years, or pay any attention to them, but just make a diligent effort in your practice. Be like the Rib Saint. Do not have any regrets about this present fleeting life, which is no more than a handful of earth from a cemetary, and do not look backwards at it. If you do not carry out your resolution, who is going to pity whom? You should try to see just how quickly this ownerless corpse is aimlessly scattered on the wild fields.

The sixth patriarch, Hui-neng, was a woodcutter in Hsinchou. He was quite unlearned. He lost his father when he was young, and he was reared and cared for by his aged mother. He made a living from the woodcutting his father had done in order to care for his mother. One day, at a crossroads, he heard a passage being recited from the *Diamond Sutra*, and he left his mother at once and began to seek the Dharma. He was a man who is rarely seen, a preminent follower of the Way. Perhaps it was easy for Hui-k'o to cut off his arm in search of the Dharma, but this cutting off of the bonds of love must have been extremely difficult, for I think that abandoning love for one's parents in this way is not easy. For eight months after he joined Hung-jen's group on Mt. Huang-mei, he neither slept nor rested, but pounded rice all night. As a result, he was correctly transmitted Hung-jen's Dharma in the night. Even after receiving the Dharma, he walked with the same mortar on his back and pounded rice for eight years. Even though he became the chief priest of a monastery and a preacher of the Dharma for people, he did not get rid of the mortar. This is indeed rare continuous practice in this world.

Ma-tsu of Chiang-hsi did zazen for twenty years. Thus, he received *inka* from Nan-yüeh. Even when he succeeded Nan-yüeh and taught the Dharma to others, he was still never negligent about doing zazen. He set an example for those who were learning Zen for the first time, and when it was time for work, he started to work first. Even when he grew old, he did not neglect this. Those of the famous present-day Rinzai tradition are descended from Ma-tsu.

Yün-yen and Tao-wu practiced together on Mt. Yo, made a vow together and for forty years, until they died, hardly ever reclined in a prone position and slept, but continued to practice the Way singlemindedly. In this way, they transmitted the great Dharma to the great master Tung-shan Wu-pen. Tung-shan said, "I wanted to practice the Way and do zazen a little, and already I have twenty years worth." This has been passed down to the present time.

When the great master Hung-chüeh of Yün-chü Mountain was staying in the Three Peaks Hermitage, a celestial being would send him food out of respect. The master visited Tung-shan, was enlightened in the great Dharma, and again returned to his hermitage. Again, the celestial being brought food, and though he called on the master, for three days he could not see him. The master no longer needed the help of this celestial being and tried only to attain the Buddha Dharma. You should think about the constancy of his determination to practice.

After Zen master Pai-chang had been Ma-tsu's attendant, there was not a day up to the day he died when he did not exert himself of behalf of those studying under him. As for the precedent he left us in his saying, "A day without work, a day without eating," Pai-chang was already an old man when he said this and had undergone many years of strenuous practice. Still, he worked hard in the fields with the younger men in training. The monks lamented over this and felt sorry for him, and they tried to make him stop working, but he would not stop. One day when Pai-chang was working, a monk hid the tools he was using and would not show them to the old master. So for that whole day, the master did not eat, because he was disappointed in not being able to join the monks in the fields. This is the story behind his "A day without work, a day without eating." In present day Sung China, in the tradition of Lin-Chin and in all monasteries everywhere, many constantly put into practice this deep teaching of Pai-chang.

While Ching-ch'ing was serving as chief priest at a certain monastery, a guardian spirit of the earth was never able to see his form. The reason was that he couldn't detect the whereabouts of the chief priest while he was working.

Zen master I-chung of Mt. Shan-p'ing had also previously received food from a celestial being. However, after the master saw Ta-tien (Pao-t'ung), the celestial being could not see him when he looked for him. The chief priest, the later Ta-wei, remarked, "I have eaten the food of Mt. Wei for twenty years, but because every bit of it went back into the latrines of Mt. Wei, I did not take a thing. I did not even follow the teachings of Mt. Wei. I am not such a simpleton as to take the guidance of others. I just worked as a cowherd for twenty years, taking care of a water buffalo bull." You should understand that he was able to take care of this water buffalo through his twenty years of continuous practice on Mt. Wei. This master had formerly studied under Pai-chang. Just quietly picture to yourselves the circumstances of these twenty years of practice and do not forget them. Even though there are some who cultivate the Way of Mt. Wei, not receiving the teachings of Mt. Wei at all and continuously practicing the Buddha Way through work is truly rare.

The great master Chen-chi Ts'ung-shen, of Kuan-yin temple in Chao-chou, was sixty-one years old when he first aroused the thought of enlightenment and resolved to seek the Way. He went on a pilgrimage carrying a priest's staff and a bowl for cleaning himself, and walking everywhere, said to himself, "If I meet someone who is superior to me, even if she is a seven-year-old girl, I will ask her for the Way, and even if he is a hundred-year-old man, if he is my inferior, I will teach him. He studied Nan-chüan's Dharma and practiced for twenty years. When he was eighty, he became chief priest of the Kuan-yin Temple, where he was the guide for the world for forty years. During that time, he didn't send a single letter to any of the families who supported the monastery in order to get donations. The meditation hall was not large, nor were there even any stands in front and behind the hall where the monks could wash their faces and so on. One time, a leg of his seat broke off. So Chao-chou bound a piece of partially burned wood to the seat and kept it like this for a long time. The monk in charge of these matters wanted to replace the leg of the seat, but Chao-chou refused. You should make the traditions of these excellent Buddhas and patriarchs models for your own lives.

It was after he was eighty that Chao-chou became chief priest at Kuan-yin Monastery in Chao-chou, and after his master instructed him in the Way, he correctly transmitted the Buddha Way. Everyone called him the "Old Buddha." Those who did not correctly transmit the Buddha Way must have been weaker than this master as far as the Dharma is concerned. Those who were not yet eighty years old must have been stronger and healthier than the master. Now, when we compare ourselves, who are strong and healthy, to this old teacher, we certainly do not come up to his standards with respect to the Buddha Way. Therefore, we must be diligent in our practices and practice continuously.

For forty years Chao-chou did not store up worldly goods, and every day he lacked sufficient rice. So, he either gathered chestnuts and ate them, or else he ate food given to him by the monks. Truly, all these are excellent examples of the lives of our predecessors, and excellent examples of practice by the Buddha's disciples. Once, Chao-chou said to the monks, "If you do not leave the monastery for your whole life and do not say a word for five or ten years, no one will be able to call you wicked. On the contrary, even all the Buddhas will not be able to call you anything."

These are golden words which illustrate continuous practice. You should understand that even though you may seem to be stupid because you are silent for five or ten years, you may be silent, but people will not call you wicked, and this is because of the merits of not leaving the monastery. This not leaving the monastery for your whole life is itself the very form of continuous practice. The Buddha Way is like this. But when you do not hear the sound of the Buddha's teaching, this is not to be considered the same as the non-evil of silence. But the supreme wonder of continuous practice is nothing other than not leaving the monastery, and not leaving the monastery is the total expression of dropping off mind and body. Stupid people do not understand this non-evil, nor do they make it known to others, because they cannot hear the Dharma preached within silence. The reason they do not teach this non-evil of silence is because they are deluded themselves. Those who do not understand that this is non-evil and do not teach it are to be pitied. The continuous practice of not leaving the monastery should be continuously practiced quietly. Do not just go about willy-nilly as if blown about by the east wind or west wind. If you possess the merit of continuous practice of not leaving the monastery for five or ten years to the extent that you do not even notice the spring breezes or autumn moon, you will be emancipated from the spring breezes and autumn moon. The realm of this continuous practice is unknown by us, and we do not understand it. This present moment of continuous practice should be engraved on your hearts as something to be greatly prized. Do not think that this silence is useless and empty. Entering the monastery and doing zazen in silence, or leaving the monastery and going all about are both the form of the continuous practice of the monastery. This continuous practice of not leaving the monastery is the realm of freedom from conditions, in the same way that the sky is free from the tracks of flying birds; it is the realm where one is completely one with the whole universe. The whole universe is the monastery.

Ta-mei Mountain is in the prefecture of Ch'in-yüan. The person who founded the Hu-sheng Monastery was the Zen master Fa-ch'ang. He was from Hsiang-yang. Once he paid a visit to Ma-tsu and asked him, "What is the Buddha?" Ma-tsu replied, "The mind just as it is is the Buddha." Thereupon, Fa-ch'ang was enlightened. Then he went to the top of Ta-mei Mountain, where he stayed in a grass hermitage far away from people. He ate the seeds of cedar trees and wore the leaves of lotuses which grew abundantly in a pond on the mountain. There he did zazen and struggled for more than thirty years. Though he was lacking in worldly things, he never concerned himself and he completely forgot time. He was aware of nothing but the alternating greening and yellowing of the mountains all around him. When you think about it, this life of great poverty was pitiful.

When the master did zazen, he placed an eight-inch high iron pagoda on top of his head, as if he were wearing a crown. He did this so that he would have to stay awake in order to prevent the pagoda from falling to the ground. This pagoda is still at the monastery of Hu-sheng, and it is taken out from time to time and serves as a memento. Up to the time of his death, the master never forgot this practice.

When many years had passed, a monk who was studying

with Zen master Yen-kuan (Ch'i-an) came to the mountain and poked about with his travelling staff, and becoming confused about where the path was, without being aware of it stumbled upon the master's hermitage. Consequently, without intending it, he met the master. He asked Fa-ch'ang, "Chief priest, how much time has passed since you began living here in these mountains?" The master replied, "All I know is the green and yellow of these mountains." Again the monk asked, "Which direction is the path out of these mountains?" The master answered, "Just follow the stream." The monk thought that this was a wonderful answer, and when he returned to Yen-kuan and told him abou it, Yen-kuan said, "Long ago, when I was in Chiang-hsi, I happened to meet a monk like that, but afterward, I heard no more about him. I wonder if this is the same monk?" Thereupon he sent a monk to ask the master to come down from the mountain, but Fa-ch'ang refused to come. So, Yen-kuan composed a poem and sent it to him. The poem read,

> The stump of the dead tree stands in the
>     cold forest;
> Even if it is exposed to the spring warmth,
>     its heart is not moved.
> Since no one takes notice of it, it being so
>     stiff and hard,
> Perhaps the carpenter will not want to use
>     it.

Once more, Fa-ch'ang did not accept the invitation. Then he decided to move deeper into the mountains, and he composed a poem, which said.

> One cannot cut all the lotuses in the pond;
> One cannot eat all the pine seeds.
> Since the world has discovered my
>     dwelling so easily,
> I shall move my hermitage deeper into the
>     mountains.

Later, Ma-tsu had a need to know the extent of Fa-ch'ang's attainment, so he sent a monk to find out. The monk asked Fa-ch'ang, "O Chief Priest, since you studied under Ma-tsu earlier, what principle did you acquire, and why did you come to live in these mountains?" The master replied, "My teacher, Ma-tsu, told me that the mind just as it is is the Buddha, and that is the reason I live here in these mountains." The monk said, "But recently the Buddha Dharma has changed." "How is it different?" asked Fa-ch'ang. Said the monk, "Nowadays, Ma-tsu says that it is neither mind nor the Buddha." To this, the master exclaimed, "That old fellow is still pulling the wool over everybody's eyes, eh? He can do whatever he wishes with this business of 'neither mind nor Buddha,' but all I care about right now is 'The mind is the Buddha.' " The monk returned to Ma-tsu and told him about all this, and Ma-tsu said, "The fruit of the plum is ripe."[6]

The whole world knows about these events. T'ien-lung was the excellent disciple of Zen Master Fa-ch'ang. Chü-tzu was another Zen man who dipped deeply into Fa-ch'ang's stream. Kya-chi, the Korean monk, transmitted the master's teaching and became the first patriarch of Zen in Korea. Consequently, everyone in the Zen tradition in Korea these days is drinking from the long stream of this master.

Even prior to his birth, a tiger and an elephant became the master's attendants, and they never quarrelled together. When the master died, the tiger and elephant carried rocks and mud and made a tomb for the master. This grave still exists at Hu-sheng Monastery. This master's continuous practice is praised unanimously by people who call him a preeminent master of past and present. Those who are slight in intelligence do not understand that this is to be praised. To think that it is all right to covet fame and fortune in the Dharma is the stupid idea of shallow people.

The Zen master Fa-yen, of the Monastery of the Five Patriarchs, said, "When my own master Pai-yün Shou-tuan, first went to live on Yang-ch'i Mountain, the rafters of the old building were badly damaged, and the rain came through, and the wind was severe. One winter night, the rooms of the monastery were completely ruined. The monks' quarters were damaged and rain and hail covered the floor, making an intolerable situation. A white-haired old monk had to wipe the snow off the top of his head. The old monk, whose eyebrows had grown long, seemed to gather together all the furrows of his large, sad forehead in the face of this difficulty. When the other monks saw him, they too felt justified in feeling sad, and they were not able to do zazen. A monk wanted to rebuild the monastery, but Pai-yün rejected the plan. "Our great teacher, Śākyamuni, said that all things are impermanent. Even the high peaks and deep valleys change. All things are just like thoughts, so how can they satisfy? And it is just so. Ancient worthies practiced on the ground under trees. This is an excellent custom of ancient times. They are the exploits of ancient wise men. When we look back on the practices of the five patriarchs, our own practices do not equal theirs. The time when one is able to practice is a mere forty or fifty years. Who has time to build a splendid new building?" Consequently, he paid no attention to the monk's request.

The next day, Fa-yen went to the Dharma hall and spoke to the monks. "When he first went to Mt. Yang-ch'i, the rafters and walls were shabby and the beds were wrapped in jewel-like snow, the cold wind shrivelled his head, and he sighed in the night, but he recalled that the Buddha had carried out his own practice beneath trees and on rocks." Consequently, Pai-yün Shou-tuan did not approve rebuilding the monks' hall. However, in spite of this, all those under the heavens who wished to practice wanted to be included among his disciples. It is delightful that so many people aspired so deeply to practice the Way. You should therefore inscribe these words on your livers.

Zen Master Fa-yen once said, "Practice does not transcend thought; thought does not transcend words." You should give these words serious consideration. "Day and

night think of it; morning and evening do it" does not mean
that you should be restless, as if you were being blown about
by the winds of the north, east, south, and west.

The palaces of Japan's emperor and courtiers are simple
dwellings thatched with miscanthus; they are not at all splendid palaces. How much less should those who have made
their home departure and study the Buddha Way peacefully
live in fine houses! Those who have acquired fine dwellings
are leading lives of error; those who are pure are rare indeed.
It is a different matter if they were owned originally, but you
should not try to obtain such a dwelling. The ancient worthies lived in grass-thatched or miscanthus-thatched houses,
and that is all they wanted. These are excellent facts. The
Ch'in Emperor Hsiang Shih-tzu says in his *Shih-tzu,* "When
you look at the conduct of the Yellow Emperor, look at his
combined palace. When you want to look at the conduct of
Yao and Shun, look at their palaces. The palace from which
the Yellow Emperor ruled the country was thatched with
grass and was called the combined palace. The palace from
which Yao and Shun ruled the country was thatched with
grass, and this was called a palace." O disciples, you must
understand that these palaces were both thatched with grass.
When we compare ourselves now with the Yellow Emperor
or Yao and Shun, we are as far apart as heaven and earth. They
made grass-thatched dwellings their palaces; how can those
who have left the home life live in fine houses and halls?
Indeed, it is a disgrace. The ancients lived beneath trees and
in forests, and this included both home dwellers and monks,
for both desired to live this way. The Yellow Emperor was the
disciple of the Taoist master Kuang-ch'eng, who lived among
the crags of the mountains called "K'ung-t'ung." These days,
many of the emperors and their retainers in Sung China
transmit this excellent spirit. Consequently, if ordinary people live in this manner, how can those who have made their
home departure be any less? How can they be more impure
than ordinary people?

Many of those who have been discussed up to this point received help from divine beings, but after the patriarchs acquired the great enlightenment, divine beings and spirits lost the power which allowed them to associate with the masters. You should understand this clearly. When these divine beings and spirits conform to the activities of the patriarchs, they can associate with them. However, once the masters have become enlightened and go beyond divine beings and spirits, there is no longer any means by which these spirits can see them clearly and they cannot approach them.

Concerning this, Nan-ch'üan said, "This old monk has no power of practice, and so he is easily seen by spirits." You should understand that being seen by these spirits is a result of having no power to practice. It is told that a temple guardian spirit who took the form of a servant in the T'ien-lung Monastery said once, "I have heard that Chief Priest Cheng-chio has lived on this mountain for more than ten years, but whenever I go to where he lives and try to see him, I cannot see him even if he is right in front of me." Truly, non-Buddhists and spirits not being able to see a person enlightened in that chief priest's Way is a fine example of the heritage of the patriarchs.

This T'ien-lung Monastery was originally a small monastery. While Cheng-chio lived there as chief priest, the Taoist sanctuary and Taoist nuns' monastery were removed and it became the present day Ching-te Monastery. When the master died, and the censor Wang Po-hsiang recorded the master's work, some people said, "The Zen master got rid of the monasteries which taught the teachings of the Taoists, so you should record the place as 'T'ien-lung Monastery' " (i.e., "Heavenly Dragon Monastery"). To this, the censor replied, "This is not right. It has nothing to do with the merits of the Buddhist priests." Many people praised the censor for this.

You should understand that this sort of thing should be considered a victory for ordinary people, not merits for the Buddhist priesthood. In general, after priests have entered the Buddha Way, they clearly transcend the divine beings and humans of the three worlds. You should deeply comprehend the fact that monks are not utilized by the world or seen by the world. You should thoroughly understand that the activities of body, speech, and mind, and such things as Buddhas and ordinary beings, delusion and enlightenment, and so forth, all come from your own minds.

The merits of the continuous practice of the Buddhas and patriarchs are, of course, a great effort made for the sake of gods and humans, but you still do not understand that gods and humans are helped by the continuous practice of the Buddhas and patriarchs.

When you now attempt to practice continuously the great Way of the Buddhas and patriarchs, it is not at all a question of large or small, or bright or stupid. Just always reject fame and fortune and do not be bound by inner and outer conditions. Don't idle away the time needed for practice, but rather practice in the spirit of a person trying to extinguish a blaze in his hair. Do not sit and wait for enlightenment, for great enlightenment is to be found in everyday activities such as eating, or drinking tea. Also, do not wish to transcend enlightenment, for the transcending of enlightenment is truly the jewel in the topknot. The person who lives in his old home should leave it; the person who has thoughts and desires should get rid of them. The famous person should abandon fame, and the person who has benefitted materially should get rid of his goods. The person with fields and gardens should part with them, and the person with a family should leave it. You should renounce them even if you do not possess them. What should be clear in this matter is the principle of being free from them whether you have them or not. That is the continuous practice of being free from everything, whatever it is. Simply making an earnest effort to practice continuously and to get rid of fame and fortune is the continuous practice of making the life of the Buddha eternal. This present continuous practice is nothing other than just that, just committing oneself to continuous practice for no other reason than to practice continuously. Therefore, you should love and respect this mind and body which support continuous practice.

The Zen master Ta-tz'u Huan-chung said, "It is better to go one foot than to talk ten feet; it is better to go one inch than to talk one foot." In a way, this is admonishing people of the present who are negligent about continuous practice and forget those things which are part of the Buddha Way, but it is not saying that it is wrong to talk ten feet. It just says that one foot of real effort is by far more important than talking ten feet. How could it be merely a question of the difference between one foot and ten feet? It is by far easier to talk about the difference between Mt. Sumeru and a grain of sesame. However, Mt. Sumeru is the whole of Mt. Sumeru, and the sesame seed is the whole of the sesame seed. The greatness of continuous practice is like that. These words are not just Huan-chung's words; they are words which transcend words.

The Zen master Tung-shan Wu-pen (Liang-chieh) said, "Speak what cannot be performed; do what cannot be spoken." This was this great priest's Way. Its true meaning is that action thoroughly pervades speech, and speech thoroughly pervades action. A whole day of speaking is a whole day of action. This is "practicing what cannot be practiced and speaking what cannot be spoken."

The great master Hung-chüeh of Mt. Yün-chü explained with regard to Tung-shan's statement, "When one speaks, there is no action, and when one acts, there is no speech." This does not mean that there is no speech or no action. "Speaking" means not leaving the Zen monastery for your whole life. "Action" means speaking by means of silence, as seen in the story of a certain monk who washed his head and went before Hsüeh-feng.[7] Do not be negligent about this.

Something excellent has been transmitted from ancient times by the Buddhas: "Even if a person lives for a hundred years, if he does not come to know himself as a Buddha, he is not the equal of someone who lives for only one day and is able to thoroughly comprehend it." This was not said by just one Buddha or two Buddhas; it has been taught by all the Buddhas and has been put into practice by all the Buddhas. Within the eternal round of life and death, the single day of continuous practice is the bright jewel in the topknot. It is the true self which I share. (Lit., "It is the ancient mirror which has the same life and death as me.") It is a day to be joyously appreciated. Continuous practice is delight by virtue of the power of continuous practice. If the power of continuous practice is still insufficient, and you do not inherit the bone and marrow of all the Buddhas, you will not hold the bodies and minds of all the Buddhas in high esteem, and you will not rejoice at seeing all the faces of the Buddhas. The enlightenment of all the Buddhas does not go away, it goes according to the suchness of things, and it comes according to the suchness of things. Although it does not come, we shall still inherit it by means of this one day of continuous effort.

Therefore, one day should be valued and respected. A hundred years lived idly is a hundred years to be regretted. It is a shambles to be deplored. However, though you are wastefully enslaved to a hundred years of just running about here and there, if you involve yourself in continuous practice for just one day, you not only practice for a hundred years of this one lifetime, but you also help the hundred years of the next lifetime. This life of one day is a life to rejoice in. Because of this, even though you live for just one day, if you can be awakened to the truth, that one day is vastly superior to an eternal life. Therefore, people who are not yet enlightened should not waste this one day. This one day is a priceless jewel which we should value highly. You cannot compare it even with a huge jewel. Do not replace it even with a dragon jewel. The ancient wise men valued this one day even more than their own lives. Surely that is something to think about. The dragon's jewel can be sought. The huge jewel may be right in your hand. However, if this one day in the lifetime of a hundred years is lost, will you ever get your hands on it again? Whatever skillful devices you may employ, there is no historical example of someone recovering a day which has passed. Wastefully spending a day is wastefully spending time which is ours. For this reason, ancient wise people valued time more than their own bodies or more than their native soil. Spending time wastefully is being seduced by the fame and fortune of this transitory world. Not spending time wastefully is being within the Way, it is activity done for the sake of the Way. As for those who are already enlightened, they will not spend even one day wastefully. They earnestly act for the sake of the Way, they speak for the sake of the Way. For that reason, we can understand why none of the Buddhas of the past squandered even a single day of practice. You must always keep this in mind. Think of this when you sit beside a bright window, leisurely spending a spring day. Do not forget it while you sit in a thatched house on a quiet, solitary, rainy night. Is it the light and dark which rob us of practice? They do not steal just a day. They pilfer away the merit of many ages to come. What enmity exists between us and the light and shade? Truly it is a bitter thing, but our neglect of practice is something we should blame ourselves for, though we do not reproach ourselves. The Buddhas and patriarchs were not without thoughts and desires, but they got rid of them. The Buddhas and patriarchs were not above ordinary conditions either, but they freed themselves from them. Though we may somewhat regret those conditions which are found within and without us, we do not utterly regret them. Consequently, if we do not abandon thoughts and desires, they will abandon us. If you very much regret your thoughts and desires, get rid of them. Truly, regretting thoughts and desires very much means getting rid of them.

Chief Priest Huai-jang, who was the Zen master Ta-hui of Nan-yüeh, practiced at Mt. Ts'ao-ch'i, where for fifteen years he served the sixth patriarch. He inherited the Way in the manner in which water is transferred from one bucket to another. The practice of predecessors such as these should be highly respected. There must have been many things among those fifteen autumns of varied activity which may trouble us. However, the fact that he did zazen and earnestly learned the Way is now a mirror for those who continue after him. There were no coals in the stove in the winter, and on autumn nights when he had no lamp, he faced the bright window and did zazen, and though this has not been widely known, it was unconditioned, absolute learning. We should consider it to be the essence of continuous practice.

Generally speaking, if we cease being attached in our hearts to fame and fortune, daily things such as eating or drinking tea become the accumulation of continuous practice. Do not forget this. Zen Master Huai-jang's statement, "Though you may talk about the realm of great enlightenment, words cannot reveal reality, for language is just concepts. The realm of great enlightenment is real, it is experience. That realm was acquired for the first time [by Śākyamuni] after eight years of continuous practice," is a rare thing either in the past or in the present. But it is the continuous practice which both the wise and the ignorant should aspire to.

When the Zen master Chih-hsien was practicing with Ta-wei, he tried to say something that would indicate his enlightenment, but he could not say a single word. This grieved him, and he burned up all his books and spent several years as a waiter-monk in the monks' hall. Later, he climbed Mt. Wu-tang and sought the whereabouts of Nan-yang Hui-chung. There, he built a hermitage of grass, cut his connections with the world, and lived a peaceful life. One day, when he was sweeping the path, a stone flew and struck a bamboo, and when he heard the sound, he was immediately enlightened. Later, he became head monk at Hsiang-yen Monastery, and all he ever owned was one bowl and one set of robes, and he did not ever exchange them for new ones while he was head monk. With no one for companions except the strange rocks and a stream of clear water, he lived an inconspicuous life in tranquillity. It is said that once he entered the mountains, he never again came down. The traces of this continuous practice are transmitted to this day at Wu-tang Monastery.

The great master Hui-chao (Lin-chi I-hsüan) of Lin-chi Monastery was the legitimate heir of Huang-po, and he spent three years as Huang-po's disciple. He followed the Way single-mindedly and followed the teaching of Ch'en-tao Monastery in Mu-chou. Three times he asked Huang-po about the great meaning of the Buddha Dharma and its fundamental ideas, and altogether he was thrashed sixty times with the *keisaku*. He burned with a fiery spirit for seeking the Way. Then he visited Kao-an Ta-yü and had a great satori, but it was really due to the two Zen masters, Huang-po and Ta-yü. It has been said that the best of the patriarchs were Lin-chi and Te-shan, but how can Te-shan be put in the same category with Lin-chi? Truly, the Zen man Lin-chi was without an equal in the whole crowd. But the Zen world of that time was more preeminent than that of today. It is said that they practiced earnestly and that they were preeminent in continuous practice, but though we may attempt to resolve the question of the extent of their continuous practice, we ought not bother to do it.

When Lin-chi was at Mt. Huang-po, while he was planting some cedars and pines one day with Huang-po, Huang-po asked him, "Why on earth are we planting so many trees right here in this deep valley?" Lin-chi answered, "First, to improve the scenery around the monastery. Second, to serve as a guide for those who come after us." Now, Lin'chi's idea was that ordinary events are not imitations. He wanted to actively show the original face in continuous practice and to be a guide marker for the continuous practice of others, and crossing swords with Huang-po was a sign he raised. Lin-chi held up a hoe before Huang-po's face and twice struck the ground forcefully with it. At this, Huang-po just raised his staff. "I have raised my staff thus, but haven't you already tasted the thirty blows?" Lin-chi made a sighing sound but remained silent. "My teaching will become widely known in the world in your time," concluded Huang-po.

Therefore, you should understand that when he planted trees even after acquiring the Way, Lin-chi personally held the hoe in his in his own hands. Huang-po was not mistaken when he said that his teaching would flourish in the world in Lin-chi's time because of this. These old precedents of men who practiced the Way by planting pines are still being transmitted today. Huang-po and Lin-chi both planted trees. During Huang-po's time, he left all the monks who followed him and became involved in the general work at Ta-an Monastery, where his continuous practice consisted of sweeping out all the rooms. He swept the Buddha hall and Dharma hall. But it was not continuous practice done for the sake of sweeping out the mind, nor was it continuous practice performed in order to cleanse the light of the Buddha. It was continuous practice done for the sake of continuous practice. It was about this time that he met the government official P'ei-hsui, who became Huang-po's disciple.

Emperor Hsüan-tsung was the second son of Emperor Hsien-tung. He was intelligent and wise from the time he was small. He loved to sit in the cross-legged position. While he was at the palace, he always did zazen. Mu-tsung was his elder brother. When Mu-tsung ascended the throne, Hsüan-tsung would playfully sit on the throne and pretend to greet the officials after the early-morning affairs of state had been concluded. When the court officials saw him do this, they thought he was crazy, and they told Mu-tsung about it. He went to see for himself and praised Hsüan-tsung: "My brother is the superior heir in this family." At the time, Hsüan-tsung was only thirteen years old.

In 814, Mu-tsung died. Mu-tsung had three sons: Ching-tsung, Wen-tsung, and Wu-tsung. Ching-tsung died after occupying his father's throne for only three years. Wen-tsung is said to have been on the throne for only one year and was

forced to abdicate by close associates. So Wu-tsung became
Emperor and Hsüan-tsung did not, and Hsüan-tsung stayed
in his nephew's country. Wu-tsung always called him his
"crazy uncle." Wu-tsung was emperor from 841 to 846. He
was the one who persecuted Buddhism at that time (845).

One time, Wu-tsung called his uncle and, in order to
punish him for getting up on his father's throne as a boy, hit
him a strong blow. Afterwards, he revived him in the garden
by urinating on him. Hsüan-tsung thereupon left the land of
his father, shaved his head, and became a novice monk under
Zen Master Chih-hsien. However, he had not yet taken the
complete precepts of the monk. He travelled about in many
prefectures with Chih-hsien, and finally they arrived at Mt.
Lu. Chih-hsien, taking a waterfall as his theme, composed
this verse:

> Dragon waters bore into the cliffs and
>     scrape away the rocks,
> But they do not ever hate their labor.
> When you see it from afar,
> You fully know how high the dragon's
>     mouth is.

He was testing the novice monk with this verse in an attempt
to see what kind of person he was. The novice continued the
verse:

> Can the water in the valleys ever stop and
>     rest?
> When the water finally reaches the sea, it
>     becomes great waves.

When Chih-hsien heard these lines, he knew the novice
monk was not an ordinary person.

Afterwards, Hsüan-tsung became the disciple of the National Teacher Yen-kuan Ch'i-an of Hang-chou, who made
him a secretary-scribe. Zen Master Huang-po was made Yen-
kuan's chief priest at that time. Consequently, Hsüan-tsung

and Huang-po sat side by side in the meditation hall. Once, when Huang-po went to the Buddha hall and bowed before the Buddha, Hsüan-tsung came and asked him, "Since the Buddha Dharma is an unobtainable Dharma which cannot be sought, and you cannot seek the Buddha, Dharma, and Sangha, why do you do this bowing?" When spoken to in this manner, Huang-po slapped the secretary with his palm and remarked gently, "I bow just because one cannot seek the Buddha, Dharma, and Sangha." To this, Hsüan-tsung answered, "Too crude." Huang-po countered this with, "There isn't a single thing within this body which seeks the Three Jewels, so how can it speak either crudely or subtly?" And once more he slapped Hsüan-tsung with the palm of his hand. Hsüan-tsung left.

After Emperor Wu died, this secretary left the priesthood and became emperor. He repealed Wu-tsung's proclamation, which caused the persecution of Buddhism, and became its protector. While he was on the throne, he always valued zazen. When he was no longer emperor, he left his father's land again and visited the distant valleys of Mt. Lu, where he earnestly did zazen. It is said that after he left the throne, he did zazen day and night. Truly, with his father dead, brothers dead, mistreated by his nephew, and so on, he seemed to be in a pitiful situation. However, his diligence in the Buddha Way was as solid as diamond, and he never neglected practice. Truly, all this is a splendid historical fact concerning continuous practice the likes of which are rarely encountered.

As soon as the great master Hsüeh-feng Chen-chüeh (Seppō) who was the chief priest I-ts'un, had aroused the thought of enlightenment, he began to join the groups of disciples at Zen monasteries in all localities, where he would serve as the monk in charge of eating regulations. He always carried a large wooden spoon around with him. Thus, he wandered around to various monasteries in all the localities, where he would continue his own practice by serving the monks in the capacity of *tien-ts'o* (*tenzō*). Whether pressed with work or at his leisure time, he never disliked where he was, and he never forgot to do zazen day and night. Up to the time he founded the training hall at Mt. Hsüeh-feng, he did not forget to share his life and death with zazen. While he was an itinerant priest, he visited Tung-shan Liang-chieh nine different times, and he visited T'ou-tzu Ta-t'ung three times; truly a rare seeker of the Way in this world.

In promoting the noble majesty of continuous practice among people, many people in the present time praise the exalted continuous practice of Hsüeh-feng. Even though the beginning of the search for the Way by Hsüeh-feng is no different from that of other people, the sharpness of his prajna insight and will make him far removed from all others. It was continuous practice which enabled him to do it. Disciples today ought to penetrate the depths of Hsüeh-feng's majestic continuous practice. When we quietly look back on his courage and diligence in practicing in all those places, truly, we understand that those things were the superb practice which is now being transmitted.

When you aspire to train under the enlightened masters, it is most difficult to catch any information you may be given when you inquire individually. There are not just twenty or thirty; there are hundreds and thousands of people making inquiry. Because you are studying Buddhism and seeking enlightenment under various masters, when you try out all their teachings, the sun will set and the day will completely end. Or else when the master addresses the students, they may have no talent and are utterly indifferent to the teaching. On the other hand, they may have talent, but the teacher concludes his remarks. It is indeed a rare occurrence, if you are a younger person or have started to practice late in life, to be to be able to sit on the far end of the sitting platform and hear the old-timers clap their hands and laugh to hear the Dharma taught. There are those who enter the training hall and those who do not, those who are touched by the master's teaching and acquire the Way, and those who do not. Days and nights pass faster than an arrow; the body is more delicate than the dew on the grass. Even though there is a teacher, we get trapped by circumstances, and it is a pity we are unable to train. It is also a pity that even though we try to train, we cannot find a teacher. I have seen this situation with my own eyes.

The great masters possess the insight which enables them to know whether a person is wise or unwise, but it is indeed rare that diligent disciples find a happy situation near a great teacher. Long ago, when Hsüeh-feng climbed Mt. Lu nine times and went to T'ou-tzu three times, he surely put up with a lot of trouble and discomfort. You should sympathize with this commitment to continuous practice, and you should pity those who do not practice continuously with their very bodies.

## NOTES

1. A pratyekabuddha is a person who is enlightened without the guidance of a master and who does not choose to share his understanding with others. Sometimes translated as "solitary Buddha," the pratyekabuddha is often found mentioned along with the arhat, who is also considered to be unwilling to mingle with ordinary beings and help them. Both the pratyekabuddha and arhat are thus examples of selfishness.

2. The "eight liberations" are eight forms of meditation. They are liberations in the sense that one is freed from some form of bondage in each.

3. The three parts of the canon are: 1) the collection of discourses or sermons (*sūtra*); 2) the collection of metaphysics or scholastic analysis of sutra terms and concepts (*abhidharma*); 3) the collection of monastic regulations and codes of conduct (*vinaya*). In other words, he knew all the vast collection of canonical literature.

4. The "three worlds" are the world of desire (*kāma-loka*), the world of form (*rūpa-loka*) in which desire is absent or minimized, and the formless world (*arūpya-loka*) where beings are formless. According to ancient Indian Buddhist cosmology, they are arranged vertically, with the *kāma-*

*loka* on the bottom containing the realms of man, animals, and the purgatories, as well as several classes of *deva* or celestial being.

5. These are special kinds of knowledge belonging to one who has reached the rank of arhat. They are: 1) insight into the past lives of all living beings; 2) clairvoyance, especially with regard to the future; 3) insight into the cessation of impurity.

6. Fa-ch'ang was also called Ta-mei (after the mountain where he lived), which means "great plum." Ma-tsu was acknowledging his attainment.

7. A monk lived at the foot of a mountain by himself, where he dipped water from a stream with a long-handled dipper. For many years, he did not shave his head as a monk should. Once another monk visited him and asked him, "What is the meaning of Bodhidharma's coming from the West?" The monk replied, "The stream is deep, the dipper handle is long." When his master heard of this later, he thought it was a remarkable thing to say. Taking a razor, he went to visit the unshaven monk. He asked the monk if he had indeed said such a thing, to which the monk replied that he had. So the master told him that if he was able to teach, he should shave his head. So the monk washed his head and knelt before his master, who then shaved his head. This story is recounted by Okada Gihō in volume 3 of *Shōbōgenzo shisō taikei,* p. 201 (Publishing Bureau of Hōzai University, Tokyo, 1953).

# KAJŌ

*"Everyday Life"*

Among the Buddha patriarchs, drinking tea and eating rice is everyday life. This matter of drinking tea and eating rice has been transmitted over a long period of time [since the days of the Buddha], and it is now manifested in the everyday life [of the patriarchs]. Therefore, this drinking tea and eating rice which the patriarchs do has been transmitted to the present time as the everyday life of the patriarchs.

The priest Tao-k'ai of Mt. Ta-yang asked his teacher, the Zen master T'ou-tzu, "Are the words which the patriarchs use for teaching the same as their daily life of drinking tea and eating rice? Are there any other words different from these which are used to teach people?" T'ou-tzu replied, "Well, let me ask you, since this land is governed by the decrees of the emperor, does he have any need to borrow power from the Hsia emperor Yü of ancient times, or from the Yin emperor T'ang, or from Yao and Shun?" Tao-k'ai started to speak, but T'ou-tu covered his mouth with his *hossu* and said, "When

205

you came here to ask that, you should have received thirty blows." Hearing this, Tao-k'ai experienced satori. He bowed and started to leave. T'ou-tzu called after him, "Tao-k'ai, come here a moment." But Tao-k'ai would not look back. Once, later, T'ou-tzu asked him, "Did you attain the realm of satori?" But Tao-k'ai covered his ears and left.

It is clear that you yourselves must guard and maintain these words of the patriarchs which are their daily life of drinking tea and eating rice. The plain tea and light food of everyday life are the deep meaning of the Buddha's teaching and the instructions of the patriarchs. The patriarchs prepare tea and rice, and tea and rice maintain the patriarchs. However, they do not rely on any other power than that of drinking tea and eating rice. They just do not waste the powers of Buddha patriarchs which they have within them.

You must make a great effort and penetrate T'ou-tzu's question, "Does he have any need to borrow the power of the Hsia emperor Yü of ancient times, or of the Yin emperor T'ang, or of Yao and Shun?" On the other hand, you should also penetrate the inner meaning of Tao-k'ai's question of whether the patriarchs have any other words of instruction apart from eating rice and drinking tea, and then you must transcend this inner meaning. You should really carefully examine whether you have transcended either the affirmation or negation of this borrowing.

The Zen master Shih-t'ou (Sekitō) Wu-chi of Mt. Nanyüeh said, "I have built this grass hermitage here, and I do not have a single thing of value. After I have eaten, if I am sleepy I leisurely take a nap." Now, though the words of instruction come and go, this "after I have eaten" means that Shih-t'ou has eaten his fill of the patriarchs' words ["eating rice and drinking tea is the Buddha Way"]. Not yet having eaten is the same as not being satisfied. However, this principle called "after I have eaten I leisurely take a nap" is manifested before eating, during eating, and after eating. It is mistaken to think that after eating one does not eat rice or drink tea. To proceed in this way is appropriate study.

My teacher, the old Buddha [Ju-ching], once said to the monks, "According to an ancient koan, a monk once asked Pai-chang, 'What is the very best thing of all?' Pai-chang answered, 'Doing zazen alone on top of Ta-hsiung Peak.' You monks should not be nonplussed by this. Furthermore, you should surpass Pai-chang when you sit. If someone were to ask me now what the very best thing of all is, I would say, there is something which is extremely excellent, and do you know what in the world it is? Eating rice with the begging bowl I brought to Mt. T'ien-lung from Ching-tz'u Monastery." There is surely something very excellent in the daily lives of the patriarchs, and it is "doing zazen alone on Ta-hsiung Peak." The matter of surpassing Pai-chang is also the very best thing. However, there is something which is even better than these, and that is "eating rice with the begging bowl I brought to Mt. T'ien-lung from Ching-tz'u Monastery." The very best thing is that everything is just eating rice and drinking tea. However, "doing zazen alone on Ta-hsiung Peak" is the same as eating rice and drinking tea. The begging bowl has for its function eating rice, and the function of eating rice is the begging bowl. For this reason, the begging bowl of Ching-tz'u Monastery is the same as eating rice at Mt. T'ien-lung. When you have had all the rice you can eat, you then know what rice is; when once you have eaten rice, you are satisfied. Once you have come to know what rice is, then you eat as much as you wish; and once you are satisfied, you eat rice again. Just what is this begging bowl? I do not think that it is just something made of wood. Nor is it something made of black lacquer, nor something made of iron. It has no bottom and no opening. It can swallow the universe in a single mouthful, and the whole universe receives it with a *gasshō*.

One time my teacher, the old Buddha [Ju-ching], said in a Dharma talk at the Ching-tu Hall in Sui-yen Monastery in T'ai country, "When hungry, eat; when tired, sleep. The hearth flames will fill the sky." "When hungry" means the lives of those who have eaten rice. Those who have not yet eaten rice are the people who are not hungry yet. However, you should understand that we whose hunger is our daily life must affirm that it is ourselves who have eaten rice. "Tired" means tiredness within tiredness. It is tiredness which includes the totality of tiredness. For this reason, it is his present moment when the life of the whole body [and mind] is completely unified with the whole body. "Sleep" means sleeping with the eyes of the Buddha, the eyes of the Dharma, the eyes of insight, the eyes of the patriarchs, and the eyes of round pillars and lanterns.

My teacher, the old Buddha, once went from Shui-yen Monastery in T'ai country at the request of Ching-tz'u Monastery, in Lien-an, and before leaving he spoke in the Dharma hall:

> For half a year I ate the rice of Shui-yen
>     Monastery and always did zazen on
>     Mang Peak.
> Once while I sat, the misty clouds gathered,
>     piling up one on top of the other.
> Thunder shook the earth, and the sky grew
>     dark;
> In the capital, the spring colors, the red of
>     apricot blossoms.

The patriarchs who teach and convert in place of the Buddha do so by doing zazen on Mang Peak and eating rice. The intensive study of the Buddha's compassion and life is revealed in this life of eating rice. "Doing zazen on Mang Peak for half a year" is the same as "eating rice." How deeply piled up are the misty clouds which are dispersed by zazen we do not know; even though thunder shakes the whole earth, it is just the spring color of apricot blossoms turning deep scarlet. "Capital" means the orderliness of the scarlet blossoms. The "thusness" of these blossoms is just "eating rice." "Mang

Peak" is the name of a mountain near Shui-yen Monastery.

One time at Shui-yen Monastery, my old teacher [Ju-ching] said to the assembled monks, "The golden, wonderful body [of the Buddha] is just the daily life of wearing robes and eating rice, and for that reason, I bow to you. Each day I arise in the morning with this golden form [which is nothing but yourselves] and each night I retire with it. Ha! The preaching of the wonderful Dharma for forty-nine years by the Buddha was uncouth. How offensive of him to hold up the flower and thereby deceive himself." You must understand that the wonderful golden body of the Buddha is the same as wearing robes and eating rice. Wearing clothes and eating rice is the wonderful golden body. This is the way one experiences the Buddha Way. Therefore, my master made a bow before the monks. When I eat rice, you also bow to that eating of rice. How much better had the Buddha not held up the flower and deceived himself.

The Zen master Yüan-chih (Ta-an) of Ch'ang-ching Hall, in Fu country, once addressed the monks in the Dharma hall: "For thirty years I lived on Mt. Wei, and during that time I ate the monastery's rice and gave it back in the latrine. I did not learn the Zen of Master Wei-shan. All I did was raise a water buffalo. When he wandered from the path into the grass, I pulled him back; when he ran amuck in someone's garden, I chastised him with a whip. Now he has been tame for some time. Unfortunately he used to pay too much attention to what people said, but now, however, he has become a pure white domesticated bull. He is always right in front of me wherever I am, dazzling white all day long, and even if I try to drive him away, he will not go." We should pay careful attention to this story. The thirty years of arduous effort with the patriarch [Wei-shan] consisted of eating rice, and there was no other consideration. When you realize the meaning of this life of eating rice, you will also understand the deep meaning of raising the buffalo bull.

The great master Chao-chou Chen-chi (Jōshū) once asked a new monk, "Have you ever been here before?" "Yes, I have," replied the monk. Chao-chou then said, "Then please have some tea before you leave." Chao-chou asked another monk, "Have you ever been here before?" The monk replied, "No, I have not." "Well then," said Chao-chou, "please have some tea before you leave." An assistant of the monastery asked Chao-chou, "Why did you say 'Please have some tea before you leave' to both the monk who had been here before and the monk who had not?" Chao-chou called to the assistant, "O assistant!" "Yes," responded the monk. "Please have some tea before you leave," said Chao-chou. The "here" of this story is neither the head nor the nostrils of the patriarchs, nor has it any connection with Chao-chou. Because we transcend "here," we may say, "Yes, I have been here before" or, "No, I have not been here before." Because you contain within you the place of suchness, you may continue to speak of "have been here" and "not been here." Therefore, Ju-ching said, "What person drenched in wine in a gaudily painted mansion can ever taste Chao-chou's tea when they meet?" The everyday life of the patriarchs is nothing but drinking tea and eating rice.

# GENEALOGY CHARTS OF CHINESE ZEN MASTERS

The following lineage charts have been included in order that the reader may be able to locate in time the various individuals mentioned in Dōgen Zenji's essays. I have made charts instead of a simple list so that not only a particular individual, but also his teacher and his own students, can be located. Several points need to be noted.

1. Asterisks mark a master who is not mentioned in the essays but who is included in the charts for purposes of clarity.
2. Dots between masters indicate that there is a break in the lineage and not all the individuals between the two are given. This is for the sake of brevity and simplicity.
3. "N.D." after a master's name means "no dates," because they are unknown.
4. Japanese pronunciations of names are given in italics following the Chinese name.
5. The double line traces the Ts'ao-tung (Sōtō) lineage of which Dōgen Zenji was part. I have traced the lineage from Ch'ing-yuan Hsing-ssu, but of course the lineage extends from him back through Hui-neng to Bodhidharma and beyond to the Indian masters.

Bodhidharma n.d.

Hung-jen
*Kōnin* n.d.

Hui-neng
*Enō* n.d.

Nan-yüeh Huai-jang
**Nangaku Ejō d. 775**
*See next page for Nan-yüeh's lineage*

Nan-yang Hui-chung
**Nan-yō Echū 677–744**

Yung-chia Chen-chüeh
**Yōka Shikaku 665–713**

*Ch'ing-yüan Hsing-ssu
**Seigen Gyōshi d. 740**

Shih-t'ou Hsi-ch'ien
**Sekitō Kisen 700–790**

*Yüeh-shan Wei-yen
**Yakusan Igen 751–834**

Tao-wu Yüan-chih
**Dōgo Enchi 769–835**

Chia-shan Shan-hui
**Kassan Zenne 805–881**

Yün-yen T'an-ch'eng
**Ungan Donjō 782–841**

San-p'ing I-chung
**Sambei Gichū 768–824**

*T'ien-huang Tao-wu
**Tennō Dōgo 748–807**

*Lung-t'an Ch'ung-hsien
**Ryōtan Sōshin 782–863**

Te-shan Hsüan-chien
**Tokusan Senkan 782–865**

Hsüeh-feng I-ts'un
**Seppō Gison 822–908**

Hui-neng
*Enō* n.d.

Nan-yüeh Huai-jang
*Nangaku Ejō* d. 775

Ma-tsu Tao-i
*Baso Dōitsu* d. 778

Pai-chang Huai-hai
*Hyakujō Ekai* 720–814

Yen-kuan Ch'i-an
*Enkan Saian* 750–842

Nan-ch'üan P'u-yüan
*Nansen Fugan* 748–834

Ta-mei Fa-ch'eng
*Daibai Hōjō* 752–839

Hang-chou T'ien-lung n.d.
*Kōshū Tenryū* n.d.

Chü-chih
*Gutei* n.d.

Kao-an Ta-yu
*Kōan-Daigu* n.d.

Mo-shan *nun*

Chao-chou Ts'ung-shen
*Joshu Jūshin* 778–897

Ch'ang-sha Ching-ch'en
*Chōsha Keijin* d. 868

Wei-shan Ling-yu
*Isan Reiyū* 771–853

Huang-po Hsi-yün
*Ōbaku Kiun* d. 850

Lin-chi I-hsüan
*Rinzai Gigen* d. 867
*see last page for Lin-chi lineage*

Ch'ang-ch'ing Ta-an n.d.
*Chōkyō Daian*
*also called Ta-wei* n.d.

Ta-tzu Kuan-chung
*Daizu Kanchū* 780–860

Yang-shan Hui-chi
*Kyōzan Ejaku* 807–883

Miao-hsin *nun*
*Myōshin* n.d.

Hsiang-yen Chih-hsien
*Kyōgen Chikan* d. 840

Ch'ing-yüan Hsing-ssu
Seigen Gyōshi d. 740

Yün-yen T'an-ch'eng
Ungan Donjō 782–841

Tung-shan Liang-chieh
Tōzan Ryōkai 807–869

Yün-chü Tao-ying
Ungo Dōyō d. 902

T'ou-tzu I-ch'eng
Tōsu Gisei 1032–1083

Fu-jung Tao-k'ai
Fuyō Dōkai 1043–1118

Hung-chih Cheng-chüeh
Wanshi Shōkaku 1091–1157

Hsüeh-feng I-ts'un
Seppō Gison 822–908

*Hsüan-sha Shih-pei
Gensha Shibi n.d.

*Lo-han Kuei-ch'en
Rakan Keishin n.d.

Fa-yen Wen-i
Hōgen Buneki n.d.

Hung-chüeh
Kōgaku d. 902

Ching-yin K'u-mu
Jōin Komoku n.d.

*Yün-men Wen-yen
Ummon Bunen 864–948

Hsüeh-tou Chung-hsien
Secchō Jūken 980–1052

Lung-ya Chü-tun
Ryūge Koton 835–923

four generations

*T'ien-tung Ju-ching
Tendō Nyojō 1163–1228
||
Dōgen Kigen 1200–1253

Ching-ch'ing Tao-fu
Kyōzei Dōfu 864–937

Fa-yin Liao-yuan
Bucchin Ryōgen 1032–1098

*Ts'ao-shan Pen-chi
Sōzan Honjaku 840–901

Lin-chi I-hsüan
*Rinzai Gigen* d. 867

*Fen-yang Shan-chao
*Bunyō Zenshō* 947–1024

Tzu-ming Ch'u-yüan
*Jimyō Soen* 987–1040

Lang-yeh Hui-chüeh
*Roya Ekaku* n.d.

Huang-lung Hui-nan
*Ōryō Enan* 1002–1069

Chao-chüeh Ch'ang-tsung
*Shōgaku Jōsō* 1025–1091

Su Tung-p'o
*Sotoba* n.d.

*Yang-ch'i Fang-hui
*Yōgi Hōe* 992–1049

Pai-yün Shou-tuan
*Hakuun Shutan* 1025–1072

Wu-tsu Fa-yen
*Goso Hōen* d. 1104

Yüan-wu K'o-ch'in
*Engo Kokugon* 1063–1135

Ch'ang-ling Shou-cho
*Chōryō Shōtaku* 1065–1123

*Fo-chien Hui-ch'in
*Egon* 1060–1117

Fo-teng Shou-chün
*Shujun* 1079–1134

Ch'an-t'ang Wen-chu
*Tandō Monjun* 966–1115

*Francis Dojun Cook* was born and raised in a very small town in upstate New York in 1930. He was lucky to be an ordinary kid with ordinary parents. By means of true grit and luck, he managed to acquire several academic degrees and learn something about Buddhism. More luck in the form of a Fulbright Fellowship enabled him to study in Kyoto, Japan, for a year and a half, where he would have learned more had he not spent so much time admiring temple gardens. He now teaches Buddhism at the University of California, Riverside, and is director of translations at the Institute for Transcultural Studies in Los Angeles. He remains ordinary, but to his credit it can be said that he raised four good kids, has a great love for animals, and cooks pretty well. A sign that at last he is growing more intelligent is that he became a student of Maezumi Roshi several years ago, the best thing he ever did. He is also the author of *Hua-yen Buddhism: The Jewel Net of Indra*, and of various articles on Buddhism in scholarly journals.

—F.D.C.

This logo is the trademark of Center Publications, publishers of fine books on Zen, Buddhism, the arts, spiritual growth and human potential, including works both classical and contemporary. Director: John Daido Loori. Editor: Stephan Ikko Bodian. Production and Design: Larry Watson.